Spies, Bombs, and Beyond

A Walking History of
Washington DC's Tenleytown

Mark Fitzpatrick

Mark Fitzpatrick
Dec 2020

Spies, Bombs, and Beyond: A Walking History of Washington DC's Tenleytown is a work of nonfiction by Mark Fitzpatrick.

Published in Washington, DC.

Printed by Minuteman Press, Ham Lake, in Ham Lake, Minnesota.

To contact the publisher: FitzpatrickDiplomacy@Yahoo.com

Copy editor: Kyle Hawke

Book designer: Katie Lawrence

Cover designer: Kyle Hawke

The cover mural, painted on a building on Grant Street and Wisconsin Avenue by Jarrett Ferrier in 2017 and produced by Stephen Voss and Charlene Kannankeril, depicts various landmarks and local connections, including several featured in stories in this book. From top left clockwise: DC flag, DC boundary line, water tower, fire station, streetcar, Continuity of Government Tower, Jesse Reno School, Abe Lincoln visiting Fort Reno in Civil War, Kermit the Frog, altitude of the DC highpoint, logo of Janney Elementary School, logo of Murch Elementary School, concert at Reno Park, WAVES operating cryptograph machine, Metro map showing Tenleytown-AU stop.

ISBN: 978-1-7359933-0-0

Library of Congress Control Number: 2020920436

For my dearest, Kyoko

Contents

Map of Stories

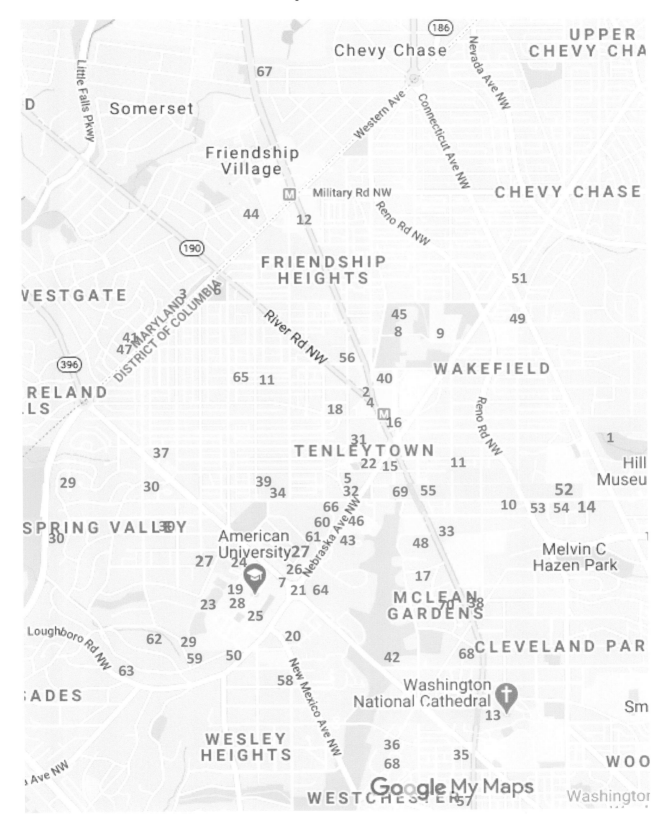

Introduction

In retirement, I had been using my time to prepare lectures about the history and politics of cruise ship destinations around the world. When the ravaging coronavirus stopped international travel in spring 2020, I turned to local sites, setting out each day in a different walk from our home in the Tenleytown/ American University Park area of northwest Washington, DC. Finding so much to see and learn, I decided to write about my neighborhood's rich history. For seven weeks, I daily posted narratives on Facebook about places within a half-hour walk of my home. This volume is in response to suggestions from friends that I make a book out of the postings. I revised many of the original stories and added a score more.

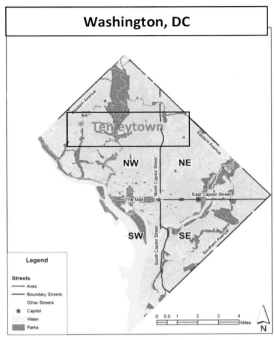

(Matt Johnson, amended by author)

Several of the stories rely on the work of local historians, particularly the late Judith Beck Helm, who in 1981 published a detailed history: *Tenleytown, D.C.: Country Village into City Neighborhood.* (A hardcover version was republished in 2000.) I was also inspired by the *Top of the Town: Tenleytown Heritage Trail,* produced in collaboration with the Tenleytown Historical Society in 2010. Part of the District of Columbia Neighborhood Heritage Trails program initiated by Cultural Tourism DC, it consists of 19 illustrated signs along a two-hour walking tour, starting at the Tenleytown-AU Metro (subway) station.

As a former US diplomat, I am particularly interested in foreign relations and the work of embassies, including by staff in the intelligence field who must pretend to be diplomats. As a concerned citizen, I am keen to understand the roots of disparities and racial cleavages in our society. The national awakening to Black Lives Matter took place while I was writing my stories. These interests are reflected in my selection of sites to write about. Tenleytown has many more places of local interest worthy of narration, but in general I sought to tell stories that also would appeal to outside audiences.

Part I: History up to a Century Ago

1. Indigenous Quarries

For over three thousand years before Europeans arrived, Indigenous people who lived around the Potomac River, often referred to as the Piscataway tribe, quarried stone near Tenleytown. Traces of ancient stone quarries have been discovered at several places in northwest Washington. The most prominent, at what is now Albemarle Street and Connecticut Avenue, is known as the Rose Hill Quarry.

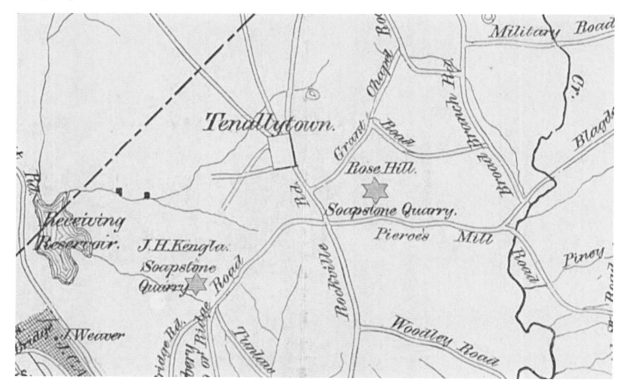

detail from Louis Kengla's 1883 map, "Localities in which aboriginal relics were found in and near the District of Columbia" (DC Public Library, Washingtoniana map collection)

The rock they quarried was soapstone, also known as steatite. It is dominantly composed of talc, which gives the stone a soapy feel and makes it relatively easy to carve. Indigenous Americans used it to make bowls, cooking slabs, smoking pipes, and other objects, but not weapons. Rose Hill Quarry was excavated in 1874 by Dr. Elmer R. Reynolds, a pension clerk and ethnologist. He found hundreds of broken pieces, several of which remain in the Smithsonian collection.

In 1890, geologist William Henry Holmes conducted further investigations of Rose Hill. He wrote: "Our excavations brought to light surprising evidences of the energy, perseverance, and skill of the ancient miner, and showed the practice of an art totally distinct from that carried on in the bowlder [boulder] quarries of Piny [sic] branch." Holmes concluded that the Rose Hill area was not used as a settlement by the Indigenous people but only for quarrying and roughing out of vessels.

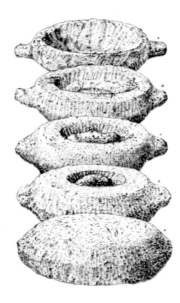

steps in the steatite-shaping process (Wayne Henry Holmes, Stone Implements of the Potomac-Chesapeake-Tidewater Province, *1897, p. 122)*

rejects from Rose Hill Quarry (Wayne Henry Holmes, Stone Implements of the Potomac-Chesapeake-Tidewater Province, *1897, p. 124)*

Rose Hill was actually two quarries, on either side of Soapstone Creek, which formerly extended westward beyond where it now begins in the park just east of Connecticut Avenue. Extension of that road to this locale obliterated most of what was left of the quarry. In 1981, historian Judith Beck Helm wrote that a remnant of this south hill was visible from the alley west of the 4400 block of Connecticut Avenue. This is no longer the case.

Soapstone Valley Park, which connects to Rock Creek Park, makes for a nice hike. Walking there in spring 2020 while talking on the phone to my cousin George in Minnesota, I lost my sense of direction. George remarked that the nation's capital is not commonly regarded as having woods where a person could get lost. Well, it does, and not just metaphorically.

Soapstone Creek, Washington, DC

2. Tenleytown

Have you ever wondered what is the difference between Washington the city and the District of Columbia (DC)? Today, there is no difference. Geographically, the city of Washington is DC and vice-versa. But it was not always that way. For the eight decades beginning from 1790, when the district was established *(story 3)*, Tenleytown lay outside the Washington city limits, which ended at Boundary Street, today named Florida Avenue. Our neighborhood instead was part of Washington County, DC. The city of Georgetown was also a separate entity. They were all united by the District of Columbia Organic Act of 1871, which created a new territorial government for the whole district. (Not that this new entity had much power. Home rule for DC did not come until 1973 and, even then, the authority was limited.)

Tenleytown is the second-oldest village in DC, after Georgetown. The recorded history of the village dates to the late 1700s, when John Tennally operated a tavern that served meals (called an "ordinary" or a public house), where two main roads intersected near the highest elevation in DC.

The roads to Rockville and to Great Falls, now Wisconsin Avenue and River Road, respectively, were originally Indigenous American footpaths. Tribesmen and women who lived in a settlement on the Potomac River called Tohoga, now Georgetown, hunted game and quarried stone around here *(story 1)*. In 1755, during the French and Indian War, General Edward Braddock improved what is now Wisconsin Avenue in order to move troops toward Fort Duquesne (later the site of Pittsburgh), where the British lost the battle.

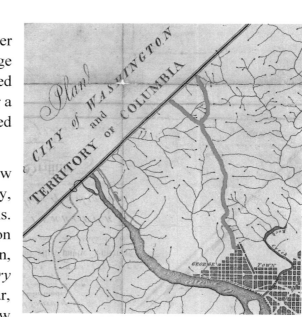

1794 map showing intersection of roads to Rockville and Great Falls (color added) (Dennis Griffith; Library of Congress, Geography and Map Division)

sketch by George Simmons, The Evening Star, *1891, Star Collection, @Washington Post, DC Public Library*

John Tennally's name is spelled various ways in old maps and documents. He probably did not know how to spell it himself. In 1776, he signed with an "X" the Maryland oath of allegiance to the United States. The small village that grew up around the tavern was called Tennallytown, which future Supreme Court Justice Oliver Wendell Holmes spelled as "TenAlleyTown" when he was stationed there during the Civil War. He apparently heard it pronounced that way by fellow soldiers who were under the impression that the town consisted of ten alleys. Later, the spelling was shortened to "Tenleytown."

Charles Dickens reportedly visited Tennallytown in 1842. As chronicled 50 years later by an American journalist, Dickens "likened its landscape to parts of north of England, and he was wont to declare that there was 'nothing finer in all England' than the scenes presented from the vicinity of Tenleytown, on what is now known as Reno Hill." But did Dickens really come to our village? Helm hints that it is possible Dickens instead was referring to the heights above Georgetown.

There is something fishy about the Dickens account. According to BBC, Dickens' first American tour did not go so well. "He began to find [Americans] overbearing, boastful, vulgar, uncivil, insensitive, and above all, acquisitive," said an English scholar. By the time Dickens reached Washington, he was in a foul mood. "I am disappointed," he wrote in a famous letter. "This is not the republic of my imagination." Washington, Dickens blasted in his *American Notes for General Circulation* travelogue, was the home of "despicable trickery at elections; under-handed tamperings with public officers; and cowardly attacks upon opponents, with scurrilous newspapers for shields, and hired pens for daggers." (*Plus ça change, plus c'est la même chose.*) Dickens then viciously satirized the United States in his next major novel, *Martin Chuzzlewit*. But his impression improved when he returned to the United States in 1867–1868. I wonder if it was during that trip that he visited Reno Hill.

Over the years, Tenleytown has seen many establishments come and go. In 1941, Sears, Roebuck & Co. erected a store here based on a Modernist design philosophy with rooftop parking. Target, the Container Store, and Ace Hardware now occupy the old Sears space at 4500 Wisconsin Avenue. The lease that Target signed in 2019 was the largest new retail lease in DC that year.

Sears was located on Wisconsin Ave. and Albemarle St. (Sears Holding Historical Archives)

Target and a condo now dominate the space

3. Boundary Marker

As we know from Lin-Manuel Miranda's *Hamilton*, the Compromise of 1790 made between Alexander Hamilton, Thomas Jefferson, and James Madison in "The Room Where It Happens" decided that the capital of our new nation would be situated on the Potomac River. This put the center of politics in the South, where Jefferson and Madison wanted it, in exchange for them supporting Hamilton's financial plan to create a national bank with the federal government assuming state debts.

author selfie at Northwest 6 Boundary Stone

Over the next two years, surveyors marked out the 10-mile-square territory, placing 40 stone markers delineating the borders with Maryland and Virginia. Today, 36 of those markers, each originally weighing a half ton, remain in place. While walking one day, I happened across Northwest 6 Boundary Stone at the intersection of Western Avenue and Fessenden Street.

The last sentence on this plaque makes the worn-out stone more significant than I first thought.

THE DISTRICT OF COLUMBIA BOUNDARY STONES

IN 1790, CONGRESS AUTHORIZED THE ESTABLISHMENT OF A TERRITORY 10 MILES SQUARE ON THE POTOMAC RIVER TO BE THE CAPITAL OF THE UNITED STATES. IT WAS PRESIDENT WASHINGTON'S RECOMMENDATION TO USE LAND ON BOTH SIDES OF THE RIVER. SURVEYOR ANDREW ELLICOTT, NOTIFIED IN 1791 TO PROCEED WITH DESIGNATING THE FEDERAL BOUNDARY BY SECRETARY OF STATE THOMAS JEFFERSON, HIRED ASTRONOMER BENJAMIN BANNEKER, A FREE BLACK MAN. TOGETHER THEY ESTABLISHED THE LOCATION OF 40 SANDSTONE MARKERS SET AT ONE MILE INTERVALS ON LAND CEDED BY MARYLAND AND VIRGINIA FOR THE NATION'S CAPITAL. VIRGINIA RECLAIMED HER LANDS IN 1846. THE STONE IN THIS PARK, SET IN 1792 AT THE TIME OF THE MARYLAND BOUNDARY SURVEY, IS NORTHWEST NUMBER 6, ESTABLISHING THE LOCATION AT SIX MILES NORTH OF THE WEST CORNER STONE. THE BOUNDARY STONES ARE CONSIDERED THE FIRST MONUMENTS ERECTED BY THE UNITED STATES.

MONTGOMERY COUNTY PARK COMMISSION
DEPARTMENT OF PARKS

4. Coaches

An advantage of living near Tenleytown is proximity to a Metro station. We will hear about that, but, first, what preceded it.

The original public transportation here was the stagecoach. In 1797, the first Georgetown-Frederick (Maryland) stagecoach ran once a week, traveling north on High Street (now Wisconsin Avenue), past Tennally's Tavern *(story 2)* at the intersection with the current River Road. This is where the Metro station now sits, and where Tenleytown got its start. By 1800, the trip was made twice a week each way, and the fare was pricey: $3.00, or 6¢ a mile. That is equivalent to $61 today for the full trip and $1.22/mile.

advertisement for the Phoenix Line stagecoaches between DC and Baltimore, circa 1835 (Library of Congress)

According to Judith Beck Helm, "Tales told by stagecoach riders between Georgetown and Frederick show they traveled always in fear of capsizing when careening down a steep hill or crossing a creek; and their worst fears often came true. … Stagecoaches frequently broke down, and passengers had to wait while an axle was repaired, or make other arrangements."

Horse-drawn cars on tracks were introduced in the district in 1862, to aid the efficiency of transportation during the Civil War. The line went from the Navy Yard (now home of the Washington Nationals baseball club) to Georgetown. In 1888, it was extended to Tenleytown.

By 1888, however, electric streetcars had already arrived in DC; then in 1890, the new electric line was extended through Tenleytown to the district boundary at what is now Friendship Heights and later beyond to Rockville.

Helm wrote: "The residents of Tennallytown were deservedly proud of their new white and blue electric cars, and the novelty of riding them never really wore off. Children were fascinated with the interiors and idolized the uniformed motormen…. It took 25 minutes to travel from Tenleytown to the

Georgetown & Tenallytown Street trolley, circa 1890 (Sellers/Copperthite Families of Georgetown 1885)

heart of the district by streetcar…. In 1901, six streetcar tickets sold for 15¢. Soon the fare was raised to 8¢ a ride."

Helm added: "Before the days when automobiles were popular, going for a ride on the streetcar was an entertainment in itself. A Saturday or Sunday afternoon, or a summer evening, was often spent riding a streetcar to the end of the line, seeing the sights along the way, and then riding back again. Some city folks would get off the streetcar at Tenleytown just to look around, perhaps pick the wild flowers, and get on the next car going back to DC."

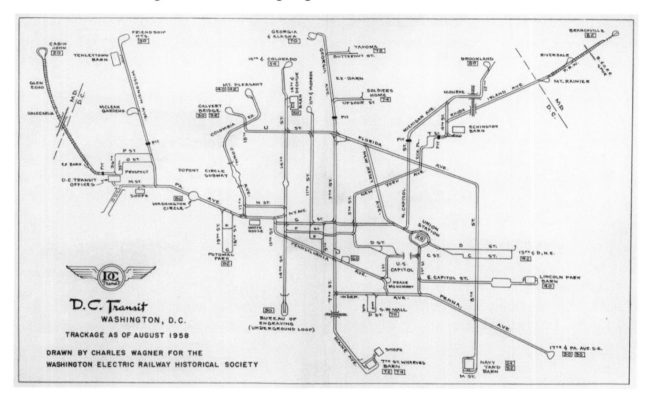

from Robert S. Crockett Streetcar Collection, 1928–1966 via Discover DC History Archive

As automobiles became more popular in the mid-20th century, streetcars became an unprofitable business. In 1956, the US Congress (which handled all administration matters for the city before the 1973 District of Columbia Home Rule Act) decreed that the trolley service had to be eliminated. The last streetcars in DC ended service on January 27, 1962 as buses took over all the routes.

During this shift, in 1960, the federal government created the National Capital Transportation Agency to develop a rapid rail system for the capital. The agency approved plans for a 97-mile regional system, for which construction began in 1969. Service on the first lines started in 1976. The Tenleytown station opened in August 1984, along with the completion of the Red Line to north Bethesda. The name was later changed to Tenleytown-AU, given its proximity to American University. The Metro overall now has 91 stations and 117 miles of track. In 2021, *inshallah*, the Silver Line is supposed to reach Dulles International Airport.

The Metro could not come too soon to Tenleytown. In the early 1970s, Wisconsin Avenue was deemed one of the busiest city streets in the United States; in 1973, the block where the Metro station today sits saw 35,000

DC Trolley at Pennsylvania Ave and 17 St. SE on the last day, January 27, 1962 (CERA Members Blog)

cars passing by each day. Washingtonians like to complain about the Metro, but I personally am satisfied. The coaches and platforms are kept clean and graffiti-free and, except on weekends, the trains come frequently. In number of passenger trips, the DC Metro ranks as the second-busiest rapid transit system in the United States, after New York's.

The tracks in our neighborhood lie deep underground: 162 feet at Tenleytown, requiring a long escalator ride. The construction workers had to dig through five geological strata of fill dirt, clay, silt, sand, and gravel, before hitting a rock stratum suitable for the tunnels.

(Wikipedia Commons)

5. Dumblane

The foxes that saunter in American University Park may be descendants of critters that survived the sporting events which took place here in the 1800s. Fox hunts were organized by the "Dumblane Hunt," located at the first Dumblane estate now occupied by American University's law school off Tenley Circle. Judith Beck Helm wrote that the fashionable Dumblane Hunt "cut a wide swath in the social and sporting life of the period."

The Dumblane house was built in the first half of the 1800s, taking the name of an

fox hunt at Dumblame oak tree, circa 1900
(photo courtesy of estate of Ruth Buchanan)

ancestor's estate in Maryland. In 1905, it became a school for Immaculata Seminary, spelled "Dunblane" *(story 22)*. Six years later, in 1911, a new country estate by the same name was built just south of the old Dumblane house. Wealthy lawyer Hazen Bond established his dream house at the top of a hill with an uninterrupted view across the Potomac Valley and to the Blue Ridge Mountains, 50 miles away in West Virginia.

The new Dumblane had varicolored bricks and wide-overhang green tile roofs that made it look like it was transported from Germany. Helm wrote: "There was a full basement, with nine rooms, including wine cellar, laundry, valet's quarters, and space for storing 30 tons of coal. The other three floors comprised 17 rooms and four bathrooms." It was the first house in Tenleytown (not counting the McLeans' mansion — *story 17*) to have a tennis court, a central vacuum cleaner system, a coal elevator, an electric washer, a clothes dryer, a billiard room, an electric phonograph, and an intercommunicating system of seven telephone lines. It is listed in the DC Inventory of Historic Sites.

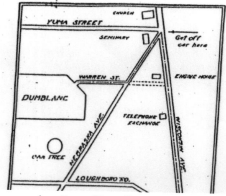

location of Bond's Dumblane
(The Craftsman, February 1913)

eastern façade of Bond's Dumblane, circa 1913
(courtesy of Elizabeth Nottingham)

The mansion is still standing today at 4120 Warren Street, where the name Dumblane remains chiseled on a cobble gate post from 1911. The estate is owned by Elizabeth Nottingham, the widow of the former executive vice president of global insurance giant American International Group. Robinson Nottingham was a naval intelligence officer in the 1960s and spent much of his career at American International Group (AIG) in the Far East. They bought the 7,000-square-foot property in 1989.

western façade of Dumblane at 4120 Warren St. today

A *Baltimore Sun* obituary in 2008 said: "Perhaps Mr. Nottingham's most daring adventure came in 1979, when he was managing AIG's Middle East operations and was sent to pre-revolutionary Iran to safeguard the company's assets as fears mounted about the toppling of the U.S.-backed shah. When the Ayatollah Khomeini was swept into power by popular revolt, Mr. Nottingham was trapped in the country for several weeks.... He escaped on the last commercial flight to leave Iran for years — carrying not just briefcases full of cash, but also deeply discounted tins of caviar he bought from an airport vendor."

Next door to the Dumblane house, at 4110 Warren Street, is a large seven-bedroom stone house with a beautiful garden, built in the 1940s. The first occupant was Indiana Senator Homer Capehart. Later, it was donated to the Catholic Archdiocese, where it has been used as a residence for archbishops, most recently Donald Wuerl, including in his retirement. Many cardinals live in Tenleytown, but this house is the only one where the other kind are found. (By tradition, the DC archbishops are named to that rank).

One might wonder why the Archbishop of Washington needs a $2.5 million mansion. According to CNN, at least 10 archbishops in the United States live in buildings worth more than $1 million, and that is not counting retired clergy. Contrast this indulgence with the asceticism of Pope Francis, who lives in the papal guesthouse in Rome rather than the grand Apostolic Palace.

Archbishop's house at 4110 Warren St.

12

6. Fort Bayard

During the US Civil War (1861–1865), the nation's capital was perched on the border with the rebel Southern states, perilously close to the fighting. After the Union lost the first decisive land battle of the war — the Battle of Bull Run in July 1861 — 68 forts were erected for protection on the perimeter of the District of Columbia. Three of them were in and around Tenleytown.

In addition, the Union prepared 93 detached batteries for field guns and several blockhouses surrounding DC. There were also 20 miles of rifle pits and 30 miles of connecting military roads. The Confederacy never captured any of these installations and most of them never came under enemy fire. They were used to house soldiers and store artillery and supplies.

Eighteen of the fort sites are managed today by the National Park Service. One of these, the earthwork Fort Bayard, stood at the corner of Western Avenue and River Road. It was named for Brigadier General George Bayard, who was mortally wounded in the Battle of Fredericksburg on December 13, 1862. The fort did not see any action.

forts defending Washington as of 1865 (Library of Congress)

7. Fort Gaines

Fort Gaines was perched on the high ground now held by Ward Circle and the American University's Katzen Arts Center. The fort saw no action but became mildly famous for the exotic 55th New York Infantry regiment that was quartered there in the winter of 1861–62. The 55th regiment was mostly comprised of French immigrants who took on the trappings of "Zouaves." The original Zouaves were Berber tribesmen from Algeria who were recruited by the French Army because of their martial reputation fighting for local rulers under the Ottoman Empire. Their image became quite fashionable. As described by Judith Beck Helm in her book about Tenleytown:

> The New York 55th 'Zouaves,' in their red jackets, stockings, and caps, shaved heads, and long swords, must have provided a fascinating sight. Colonel Elmer Ellsworth formed many Zouave units in the area, bringing an element of romance, danger, style, and even humor into the tedium of soldiering.

The French immigrants also brought culinary skills. Helm explains:

> The *Washington Star* of January 9, 1862, reports that President and Mrs. Lincoln and party attended a celebration with "the French regiment" near Tennallytown. And apparently the French cuisine served at Fort Gaines was far better than any other camp food. Unlike the usual regimental mess, the Frenchmen of the 55th New York "knew something about cooking, and their officers' mess, at least, was famous, President Lincoln dined with them... and told the officers afterward that if their men could fight as well as they could cook, the regiment would do very well indeed. They had given him, he added, the best meal he had had in Washington."

dashing New York 55th "Zouaves" Regiment posing by a cannon at Fort Gaines, 1862
(American University Archives and Special Collections)

8.   Fort Reno

The highest elevation in Washington, DC is a knoll just northeast of Tenleytown Metro station, 409 feet above sea level, with an expansive view. In the Civil War, the largest and strongest of defenses around the city of Washington was built here. It was initially called Fort Pennsylvania, having been constructed by troops from that state. In 1863, it was renamed Fort Reno to honor Major General Jesse Lee Reno, who died in battle the previous year. (Reno, Nevada was also named after the general.) The fort had three 100-pound Parrott siege guns and nine 27-pounder barbette guns. Three thousand men were stationed there.

In September 1862, troops encamped at Fort Reno joined other elements of the II Corps in marching 75 miles northwest to Antietam Creek, Maryland. There, on the 17th of the month, the two sides suffered a total of 22,717 dead, wounded, or missing in the bloodiest single day in US military history.

In July 1864, Confederate General Robert E. Lee heard from spies that DC was undermanned because Union General Ulysses S. Grant insisted that troops be moved from the capital defenses to reinforce his army at Petersburg, Virginia. Lee sent General Jubal A. Early to attack Washington from the north. When lookouts at the Fort Reno signal tower saw clouds of dust and then Confederate army wagons moving toward the city, small squadrons from Fort Reno advanced into the countryside to fend off the invaders. One of the Parrott guns hit a Confederate camp three and a half miles away.

(Library of Congress)

Seeing the power of the cannons at Fort Reno, Early decided to focus his attack on the less-well armed Fort Stevens, about three miles to the east near Georgia Avenue. There the Union prevailed, thereby saving the capital, according to some accounts. But historians say Early had no expectation of capturing Washington. In retaliation for the siege of Fredericksburg, he just wanted to plunder as much as he could, in order to try to undermine public confidence in the Union, which was already unsteady. The Battle of Fort Stevens was the only Civil War battle to take place within the district's boundaries.

9. Erased Community

After the Civil War, Fort Reno was dismantled and developers divided most of the land into small lots. Formerly enslaved African Americans who had worked at the fort and others who sought refuge joined working-class families of mixed races who were there already to build a community called Reno City. It cost $12.50 to buy a 25-by-100-foot lot.

The 52 acres comprising Reno City featured modest houses, three Black churches, a Black masonic lodge, and a Black school. Where the fort had been, the district government constructed an underground water reservoir and red-brick water tower, which still stands as the most distinctive landmark of Tenleytown.

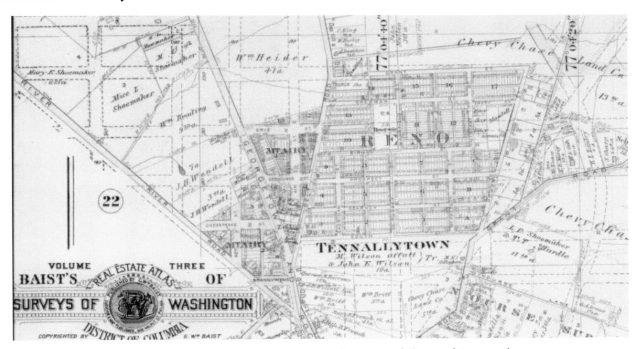

1903 map showing streets and plots of Reno City (Library of Congress)

After a streetcar line arrived, making downtown DC easily accessible, developers bought large tracts of land and planned subdivisions for middle-class white families. Developers touted the neighborhood's modern amenities: police and fire protection, electric lights, and water and sewer service. They did not tout, or like, the aging, predominantly African American Reno City. At a public hearing in 1926 about Reno, Black attorney James Neill illuminated the racism: "They... say that this is an unsightly place, that it is a blight upon the district. Why is it a blight? Simply because negroes occupy it. They want a white settlement there."

Newer, white residents were clamoring for better schools and services, which provided an excuse to condemn Reno City houses and, between 1928 and 1950, to move out the 370 mostly African American families. The land was cleared for additional reservoirs, Fort Reno Park, and two public schools for white children. Woodrow Wilson High School, built in 1935, remained predominantly white until a racial integration campaign took place in the late 1960s. With over 1,800 students, it is the largest comprehensive public high school in the district.

Helm quotes a letter that real estate agent Harold E. Doyle wrote in July 1938 to the director of planning of the National Capital Park and Planning Commission (as it was then named): "I and a number of my friends many years ago took over between 200 and 300 lots in the section for the purpose of preventing further building for colored occupancy.... My interest [is] eliminating the subdivision of 25 foot lots on 30-foot streets.... The colored folks would, I am sure, scatter."

The purposeful destruction of a middle-class Black community was not an isolated incident. It happened throughout the United States, especially when federal highways were routed to displace African American neighborhoods in Charlotte, Detroit, Miami, Richmond, St. Paul, Syracuse, and many other cities, contributing greatly to racial income disparity.

The only building remaining from Reno City is the Jesse Reno School, built in 1903 to serve Black students from kindergarten through eighth grade. By 1945, the last of the African American houses in Reno City were demolished. No Black residents were given the option to remain; all had to leave. A few Black children from elsewhere continued to attend Jesse Reno School, but it was finally closed in the early 1950s and those children had to travel to Black schools in the eastern part of the city until the city was finally desegregated. In the 1970s, the Jesse Reno School was re-opened as the Rose School for students with special needs, and in 2014 it was restored and connected to the Alice Deal Middle School, which had been built in 1930–31 on land acquired through condemnation hearings. Today the Alice Deal school is considered to be the "most coveted middle school in the district" (to quote the *Washington Post*).

Jesse Reno School, 4820 Howard St. NW, circa 1900 (Charles Sumner School Museum and Archives) and today

10. James Wormley

Writing this book at a time when many a political pundit worried about the prospect of a hung election in November 2020, I was delighted to come across a neighborhood site that is related to the most disputatious presidential selection in US history.

At 3530 Van Ness Street, an African American Heritage Trail sign marks where "celebrated hotelier" James Wormley and his brother owned two country houses on a 10-acre estate in the 1870s and 1880s. The sign says: "As a young man, the free-born Wormley worked as a jockey, a California Gold Rush 'Forty-Niner,' a Mississippi river boat steward, and in other adventurous occupations around the country. After returning to Washington, he operated a catering business, lodging houses, and a restaurant. In 1871, he opened Wormley's Hotel at 15th and H Streets, serving wealthy whites. Produce grown on the land here supplied the hotel's acclaimed kitchen." The property also had a racetrack.

 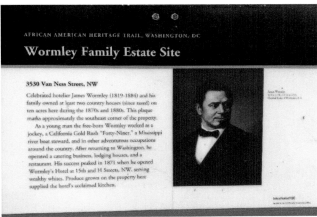

When Wormley's parents arrived in the capital in about 1815, his father Lynch engaged the services of prominent lawyer Francis Scott Key to sue for his certificate of freedom. Such a document was necessary for any free African American to engage in business within the District of Columbia. According to the White House Historical Association, "the Wormley family earned its livelihood from one of the only pursuits available to free blacks: personal service to the burgeoning community of white residents of Washington." Lynch and his sons developed a successful livery business as hack drivers to politicians and businessmen.

Wormley's Hotel, circa 1884,
DC Public Library Washingtoniana Collection

James then opened his own restaurant and hotel business at his houses near the White House. In 1867, a delegation from Japan stayed at his houses for their entire six weeks' stay in Washington. His fortunes prospered to the extent that he bought and extended the building that became the cornerstone of his hotel business.

Wormley's Hotel was a favorite of politicians. As described in a 2001 *Washington Post* article, the hotel was famous for its well-managed room and world-class cuisine, and "boasted not only an elevator but also one of the capital's first telephones." John Philip Sousa conducted the Marine Corps band at some banquets there.

Of greatest historical interest, the hotel was the site of a secret deal, known as the Compromise of 1877, that swung the electoral college vote in the hotly contested 1876 presidential election to Republican Rutherford B. Hayes. In return, Hayes's negotiators provided assurances to the southern Democrats that federal troops in Louisiana, South Carolina, and Florida would be withdrawn, effectively ending Reconstruction.

The deal ended a months-long stalemate over the election results and quelled the mood of anarchy that was rising in the capital over what was seen, with some reason, as a stolen election. There were threats of violence, harking back to the 1874 Battle of Liberty Place in New Orleans, during which Black federal troops were employed in an effort to suppress a white supremacist militia intent on overthrowing the state's Reconstruction-era Republican Party government. In 1876, Hayes had lost the popular vote but prevailed in the electoral college by a one-vote margin, based on contested vote counts in those three states with Republican governments.

Back to what was sometimes called the "Wormley Compromise": James Wormley was not in the room where it happened. Hayes was not in the room either but was informed of the progress of the negotiations by telegram. He soon became disillusioned by the devastating effect this decision had on Black suffrage and other civil rights in the South. He left office after one term and afterward, as if in atonement, devoted much of his energy and resources to African American education.

Wormley also was devoted to that cause. Earlier, in 1871, he persuaded Congress to fund the city's first public school for Black students. It was called the Charles Sumner School in honor of

prominent abolitionist Senator Charles Sumner. Sumner had been so close to Wormley that he gave him his personal copy of the Thirteenth Amendment (which abolished slavery).

Joe's Seafood, Prime Steak & Stone Crab restaurant now occupies the site of the former Wormley's Hotel at H St. and 15th St. NW

11.   Call Boxes

In grandson Gideon's favorite book, Mr. Frumble, seeing smoke rising in the garden next door, runs to the fire alarm box and pulls the handle. I had never seen such devices until I moved to Washington, DC, where they are ubiquitous relics. Beginning in the 1860s, police and fire call boxes were installed at street corners throughout the capital. They were connected via a massive underground network of cables.

fire box at Warren and 38th

The fire boxes, which came first, relied on a telegraph system. If you saw a fire, like Mr. Frumble, you would run down to the box and turn the key inside, which would send a message to the central alarm center. The transmission matched a location on a large map (which are also featured in the Curious George books that grandparents like to read).

The less numerous police boxes were used differently. They had telephones connected directly to the police department and were used by officers on patrol to check in, call for backup, or receive updated orders. Such call boxes were in use throughout the country until made obsolete with the introduction of the 911 emergency call system in the 1970s. Some cities, such as San Francisco, still rely on fire alarm boxes for redundancy in case of emergency.

In DC, the electronic components for both systems were removed by 1995, but many of the metal call boxes themselves remained, battered by weather, graffiti, and vandalism. Twenty years ago, the city initiated a project to refurbish these quaint reminders of yesteryear. About 700 boxes were stripped, primed, and prepared to house community art installations through a program called "Art on Call." Neighborhoods in the city decided on their own themes. In Tenleytown, 11 boxes feature watercolors of historical buildings in the neighborhood by Lena Frumin. Their locations, and those of other "Art on Call" boxes in adjoining neighborhoods, are marked by "@" in the Tenleytown map on page 32.

police box at Brandywine & 44th

12.   Friendship Heights

My family feels fortunate to live within walking distance of the shopping mecca of Friendship Heights. Lord & Taylor, Saks Fifth Avenue, Neiman Marcus, and a slew of designer boutiques including Cartier, Gucci, and Dior co-exist with bargain outlets like H&M, Nordstrom Rack, and T.J. Maxx (where we shop). I always wondered how the expensive stores could stay in business; the coronavirus pandemic has now left many of them shuttered.

In early June 2020, I joined a Black Lives Matter march that began in Friendship Heights and went south down Wisconsin Avenue to the National Cathedral. The march was similar in size to a street protest held there 48 years earlier. Whereas in 2020 we called for stopping racial injustice and discrimination, stopping radical development was the demand of the protestors in 1972. A newspaper at the time labeled Friendship Heights "the hottest piece of real estate in the United States." Demonstrations did not prevent the zoning changes that ushered in the malls that today characterize Friendship Heights.

Most of the expensive shops are located across the DC border in Friendship Village, Bethesda, Maryland. One fun fact about Friendship Village is that is has the second-highest life expectancy in the United States, at 96.1 years of age. This is not surprising if you have seen the clientele at Rodman's Discount Store at 5100 Wisconsin Avenue. This family-owned business is a Washington institution, known for its international gourmet foods and wines.

The neighborhood got its name from a former colonial estate that stretched from American University and Cleveland Park north to what is now the Bethesda Metro station. In 1713, Charles Calvert, 5th Baron Baltimore, granted the 3,124-acre tract to two colonists, Thomas Addison and James Stoddart. They called their combined estate "Friendship," to commemorate their good relations.

Friendship Heights became a thriving neighborhood after trolley tracks from Georgetown up Wisconsin Avenue reached the border with Maryland in 1890, prompting local entrepreneurs to construct homes for commuters. Stores did not arrive until several decades later.

13.   National Cathedral

The most magnificent building in the Tenleytown environs is Washington National Cathedral. Modeled on the English Gothic style of the late 14th century, it more than lives up to its name. With its gothic towers, flying buttresses, rose windows, ceiling boss stones, 10-bell peal, Bethlehem foundation stone, 400 carved angels, and 112 gargoyles, plus ten times that many smaller grotesques (including a recent one of Darth Vader), the building rivals European cathedrals in its grandeur. (Note: gargoyles are grotesques that spit — i.e., they have rain spouts.)

(Washington National Cathedral)

The National Cathedral is America's spiritual center, where we pray for peace and our heroes are put to rest. Its website says the cathedral "holds a unique place at the intersection of sacred and civic life. As the Cathedral of the Episcopal Diocese of Washington, we strive to serve God and our neighbors as agents of reconciliation, a trusted voice of moral leadership and a sacred space where the country gathers during moments of national significance."

Started in 1907 with a ceremonial setting of the foundation stone by President Theodore Roosevelt and not completed until 1990, with President George H.W. Bush witnessing the final stone placing, the cathedral was the longest-running construction project in Washington, DC.

The first service, in 1898 on the cathedral close before construction got underway, was held to dedicate the Peace Cross to mark the end of the Spanish-American War. During the four years that the United States was involved in World War II, special interfaith services were held throughout the year "on Behalf of a United People in Time of National Emergency," as the services were named. In March 1968, the Rev. Dr. Martin Luther King, Jr. preached his last sermon during a Sunday service at the cathedral; he was assassinated four days later. In early 1973, during the Vietnam War, Leonard Bernstein conducted the National Symphony in Haydn's *Mass in Time of War*; nearly 5,000 people packed the cathedral while 15,000 others listened outside in the rain.

The stained-glass "Space Window," officially named the Scientists and Technicians Window, contains a piece of lunar rock from the Sea of Tranquility, donated by the crew of Apollo 11: Neil Armstrong, Edwin (Buzz) Aldrin, and Michael Collins.

In 1987, on the eve of the Reagan-Gorbachev summit, American and Russian church leaders gathered at the cathedral for a four-day prayer vigil. In 2014, the cathedral opened its doors to Muslim Friday prayers. The National Cathedral was where Defense Secretary Jim Mattis, beginning in late 2017, came to pray and reflect on the nightmare that the United States and North Korea might soon be in a nuclear war, according to Bob Woodward's book *Rage*.

"Space window" with moon rock (Washington National Cathedral)

My strongest image of the building dates to May 2001. *The West Wing*'s "Two Cathedrals," the best episode of the best TV series ever, features a funeral for Mrs. Landingham at the National Cathedral. Afterwards, President Jed Bartlet remains before the alter alone, cursing God in Latin for the afflictions imposed on his entourage and the nation. This devout Catholic then lights a cigarette, drops it on the cathedral floor, and grinds it under his foot. "Two Cathedrals" is a metaphor for church and state: the cathedral and the White House.

The cathedral grounds include two prestigious prep schools: St. Albans School (for boys), from which Michael Collins graduated, and the National Cathedral School (for girls), with the co-ed Beauvoir School, the National Cathedral elementary school, serving students from pre-K through third grade for both schools.

stones damaged by 2011 earthquake

Although the mid-Atlantic is not known for seismic activity, in August 2011, a 5.8 magnitude earthquake shook the area, damaging many of the pinnacles, buttresses, and other architectural features of the cathedral, forcing it to be closed for several months. Fundraising for the $34 million worth of repairs needed has delayed completion.

How unfortunate that at our current time of national emergency during the coronavirus pandemic, the church doors were again closed.

14.   National Bureau of Standards

The National Institute of Standards and Technology (NIST) is one of the "obscure" federal agencies that Michael Lewis mentions in his 2018 bestseller, *The Fifth Risk*. Lewis's book describes the nitty-gritty, vital work conducted by faceless feds who are under attack by their own leaders. Lewis does not give NIST as much attention as the other agencies he lauds. He just notes that it is "stuffed with Nobel laureates" and does everything from setting the standards for construction materials to determining the definition of a "second" and of an "inch," which he notes is more complicated than you think.

NIST is headquartered in Gaithersburg, Maryland. But until the 1960s, it carried out its work at 28 buildings on the hill currently occupied by the International Chancery Center (ICC, *story 52*) and the University of the District of Columbia. Back then, it was called the National Bureau of Standards (NBS). A small park in the ICC features an apple tree descended from the one that inspired Isaac Newton's theory of gravity.

Local historian John DeFerrari writes: "The Bureau was founded in 1901, during a period of burgeoning industrial production and dramatic technological change. Telephones, automobiles, light bulbs, electrical machinery — it all needed practical, reliable standards based on methodical scientific testing. The new Bureau filled this need."

"First housed temporarily in the old Office of Weights and Measures building on Capitol Hill, the fledgling Bureau in 1901 urgently needed space to build its own laboratory. The requirements were exacting. The laboratory had to be well outside the city proper, somewhere completely free from vibration, traffic disturbances, and the electrical interference caused by streetcar lines." There, the Bureau built extremely precise measuring instruments.

National Bureau of Standards (Library of Congress)

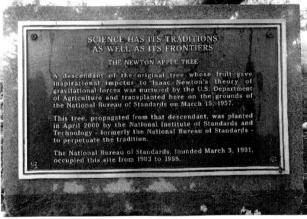

plaque under apple tree at International Chancery Center

The *National Geographic* marveled in 1915 that one thermal instrument was so sensitive it could be thrown off by the heat from the presence of its operator. Another was "so delicately adjusted that it shows the loss of weight due to the reduction of the Earth's attraction when two pieces of metal are weighed one upon another instead of side by side."

DeFerrari tells the story of when President Woodrow Wilson was invited to come out to the lab on a Sunday to see a new all-metal airplane for testing: "He, Mrs. Wilson, and Commerce Secretary William Redfield did so, but due to a misunderstanding the building was locked and no one around to open it. Determined to achieve what he had set out to do, Wilson found an open window and, with the help of Secretary Redfield, he and Mrs. Wilson boosted themselves into the lab to inspect the curious new invention."

The bureau moved to pastureland at Gaithersburg to be distant from urban distractions, like the reason it first was established on the site at what is now Van Ness Street and Connecticut Avenue. Another reason to move, offered by the bureau director in testimony to Congress, was that the Van Ness location was no longer tenable, in part because it was "extremely vulnerable in the event of an atomic attack." Well, aren't we all?

Strangely, none of the bureau's historic buildings were preserved for posterity. All I could find was a former entrance gate, pictured in the below photo on the southwest corner. A plaque near the gate put up by the Institute of Electrical and Electronics Engineers (pictured below right) reads: "The first atomic clock, developed near this site by Dr. Harold Lyons at the National Bureau of Standards, revolutionized timekeeping by using transitions of the ammonia molecule as its source or frequency. Far more accurate than previous clocks, atomic clocks quickly replaced the Earth's rotational rate as the reference for world time. Atomic clock accuracy made possible many new technologies, including the Global Positioning System (GPS)."

Intelsat used to own 14 acres on the southwest part of the old NBS grounds, but sold it to Whittle School and Studios, a newly established global educational enterprise that also recently opened campuses in Shenzhen, China and Brooklyn, New York.

former NBS entrance gate on Connecticut Avenue

15.   Fire Station!

Engine House No. 20 at 4300 Wisconsin Avenue is based in an Italian-style firehouse. It was built at the turn of the 20th century when firehouses were generally a one-of-a-kind design. Tenleytown Firehouse started off with horse-drawn equipment but in the 1920s became the district's second motorized fire station, with an additional larger bay to accommodate a self-propelled hook and ladder.

According to town boosters, the modern firehouse assured builders and buyers that Tenleytown was a good investment. Engine House No. 20 is the second-oldest of the city's 19 pre-WWII firehouses still in use today. The larger bay to the right was recently renovated in harmony with the original design. The firehouse is listed in the DC Inventory of Historic Sites.

Engine House No.20, circa 1920 and in 2020
(left photo from 100 Years of Glory, a history of the District of Columbia Fire Department*)*

pre-1920, (DC Fire and EMS Museum)

This page is dedicated to grandsons Gideon and Kenji, without whose enthusiasm I might not be as excited about fire trucks.

16. Masonic Temple

It may not be the most impressive building on Wisconsin Avenue, but it is among the most interesting. The William R. Singleton Masonic Temple at 4441 Wisconsin Avenue used to be a key institution in Tenleytown. The first masonic hall here was built in 1908–09, named in memory of a beloved former Grand Secretary of a lodge in the area. It is the home of the oldest continually operating chartered mason lodge in the district. The current structure dates from 1926 and has housed various enterprises, including a US post office, on its first floor.

Freemasonry, commonly referred to as Masonry, is the world's largest and oldest fraternity. Growing out of the medieval guilds of stonemasons in Scotland and England and taking inspiration from that craft, Freemasonry aims to "build" a better society.

To quote the DC lodge website: "Freemasonry is an initiatic society which seeks to unite men of differing races, beliefs, and backgrounds into a harmonious and productive community through the application of moral values and the practice of benevolence, intellectual development, and mutual respect." ("Initiatic" means a spiritual initiation.) While not a religion, Freemasonry has rites that are related to religion. Members must believe in the existence of a supreme being and the immortality of the soul, and they are obliged to contribute to charity.

Singleton Masonic Temple, 4441 Wisconsin Avenue

Masonry played a key role in spreading the progressive ideals of the Enlightenment. Its members, such as Wolfgang Mozart and Isaac Newton, made an enormous impact on public life. The 18th century's thinking class applied masonic principles when it led society away from revelation and faith to belief based on reason and science. Masons promoted the concept of "utility" as the foundation for right behavior. With its emphasis on voluntary association, masonry was also important to the development of civil society.

These ideas challenged the establishment. The Catholic Church has been a fierce opponent and still bans Catholics from becoming masons (although not vice-versa: Masonry does accept Catholics). Masons were charged with conspiring to undermine religion and plot revolution. They form private clubs, use arcane symbols, conduct secret rituals behind closed doors, and initiate members and promotees with passwords and secret handshakes.

The idea of masonic brotherhood probably descends from a 16th-century legal definition of a "brother" as one who has taken an oath of mutual support to another. As masons advance through various degrees, they swear to keep the contents of that degree secret and to support and protect their brethren unless they have broken the law. The tenet of Brotherly Love extends to the whole of mankind.

Mozart's opera *The Magic Flute* has been described as "an Enlightenment allegory, veiled in masonic ritual." But it does not reveal any confidences of the fraternal order. According to my wife Kyoko, who studied opera appreciation, some music scholars contend that halfway through, the plot confusingly changes because Mozart and librettist Emanuel Schikaneder realized they must not give away the secrets. Austria banned Freemasonry several years after Mozart died in 1791.

stage design for a production of The Magic Flute *in Brno in 1793; the three temples, bear the German inscriptions "Vernunft," "Weisheit," and "Natur" ("reason," "wisdom," "nature")*

This mysterious nature of Freemasonry lends itself to conspiracy theories linking it with the "New World Order" and the "Illuminati," bent on global domination or secretly in control of world politics. Freemasons were suppressed by both the Nazis in Germany and the Communists in Eastern Europe. Anti-masonry has also gone hand in hand with anti-Semitism over the years.

In the United States, George Washington, Benjamin Franklin, and many other founders, probably including Thomas Jefferson, were masons. At least 15 US presidents have been members (Gerald Ford was the last). It is widely believed that the masonic influence is apparent in the configuration of Washington, DC. The architects who designed the White House and the Washington Monument were both known masons. The city has served as the headquarters of the Scottish Rite of Freemasonry in the Southern Jurisdiction of the United States for many years.

We do not hear much about masons these days. The fraternal order has been declining in strength since its peak in 1959, when it had over 4 million American members, plus millions more overseas. Today, US membership is one million at most and many of its temples have had to be repurposed. The one on Wisconsin Avenue remains active, however; four lodges that have merged to form the William R. Singleton-Hope-Lebanon Lodge #7. Several other masonic lodges also meet there.

17.   McLean Gardens

Nearby neighborhoods are home to well-off people, but not quite like the ones in this story.

Walking down Wisconsin Avenue past the former Fannie Mae building, you come across a couple dozen red-brick buildings, built during World War II. The development is called McLean Gardens, named after a former owner of the 43-acre property, newspaper publisher and property magnate John R. McLean. The tony town of McLean, Virginia (home of the CIA), is also named after him. It was a station on his Great Falls and Old Dominion Railroad. He called his estate "Friendship," even though it lay south of the colonial Friendship land grant (*story 12*).

original stone wall and water trough for horses

ballroom and statuary from former estate

John McLean's son Edward (Ned) Beale McLean married into another fabulously rich family: his bride, Evalyn Walsh, was the daughter of a gold mine owner. As a teenager, she was sent to Paris for singing lessons, but adopted a wild life. One tale is that she applied rouge to her cheeks to affect the look of a prostitute. Back in Washington, after marrying Ned in 1908, she was a leading socialite, a confidante to Alice Roosevelt Longworth (daughter of Theodore Roosevelt) and Florence Harding (wife of President Warren G. Harding). The couple epitomized the Roaring Twenties, going on wild escapades, and entertaining in a grand style never seen before or since in Washington. Ned McLean's connection with Harding and his cabinet ruined his reputation when he got mixed up in the Teapot Dome bribery scandal. Ned falsely told Senator Thomas Walsh that he had given Secretary of the Interior Albert B. Fall a $100,000 loan when, in fact, Fall had illegally received money from private oil companies. Ned's admission of falsehood provided the "smoking gun" of the scandal.

Ned and Evalyn Walsh McLean, 1912 (Library of Congress)

Evalyn is most famous for her ownership of the Hope Diamond. She and Ned bought the 45-carat jewel from Pierre Cartier in 1911 for $300,000 (over $8 million today). Named after a previous owner, the Hope Diamond is arguably the most famous jewel in the world, with a recorded history of four centuries, dating to its origin in India. It has a rare blue color, due to trace elements of boron. Owned by King Louis XVI and Marie Antoinette before they were beheaded in the French Revolution, the diamond is said to have been cursed. This legend was amplified when Ned and Evalyn's nine-year-old son Vinson, America's most famous baby, was killed dashing across Wisconsin Avenue.

the Hope Diamond (Smithsonian, photo by David Bjorgen)

Evalyn wore the diamond almost every day and liked to make a game of hiding it on her estate during lavish parties, then inviting guests to find it. Once she lost it by putting it on her Great Dane, and another time by allowing her granddaughter to teethe on it. When she and Edward made a highly-publicized journey to Russia shortly after the October Revolution, acclaimed US diplomat William Bullitt had to talk her out of flaunting the Hope Diamond on the streets of Moscow as a symbol of the superiority of capitalism.

Upon her death in 1947, Evalyn's jewels were left to her grandchildren. However, the trustees sold them to settle her debts. The couple had burned through all of their wealth. The purchaser, New York diamond merchant Harry Winston, was persuaded in 1958 to donate it to the Smithsonian. He sent it to the institution in a box wrapped in brown paper as simple registered mail, insured for $1 million. The Hope Diamond has since been the Smithsonian National Museum of Natural History's most popular exhibit.

police call box on Wisconsin Ave. featuring portrait of Evalyn wearing the Hope Diamond

Meanwhile, Ned died in a mental institution in 1941 and the estate was sold to the government, which built dormitories and apartments to house the growing number of defense workers. The ballroom from the McLean estate remains intact, as do some of its garden features. After the war, the government sold McLean Gardens to The Hartford Insurance Company. In 1980, after a long battle by the tenants, who were able to secure the largest buy-out in DC history by a residents' association, the original apartment buildings converted to condominiums. Today it is home to many diplomats and political figures. We will hear about one of them in story 70.

18. American Creed

Walking around the neighborhood brings me past a score of houses of worship. The one in this story is not necessarily the most important, but it allows me to introduce a leading member of the congregation a century ago. With apologies, I will bury the lead.

When I commuted to work via Metro, I walked daily by St. Columba's Episcopal Church at 4201 Albemarle Street. This was the site of the first Episcopal mission in the neighborhood, established in 1875. According to a 1905 manuscript, "at that time there were certain elements in the Tenallytown settlement that presented a challenging need for missionary work." St. Columba's also covered the racially mixed community *(story 9)* that had taken root next to the Civil War Fort Reno northeast of Tenleytown. In 1899, it was decided to build a separate "Episcopal mission for colored persons" as an outgrowth of the church. The current stone structure of St. Columba was finished in 1903.

At that time, William Tyler Page, who lived just north of Tenleytown in Friendship Heights, was a vestryman and choir director at St. Columba's Church. His day job was at Capitol Hill, where he started as a page at the US House of Representatives at age 13 and worked his way up to be Clerk of the House in 1919. Although Page never attended university, he was widely read and took many correspondence courses. He was a descendant of the tenth US president, John Tyler. At his peak, Page knew more than anybody about the functioning of the legislative branch.

St. Columba's Episcopal Church, 4201 Albemarle St.

William Tyler Page, Clerk of the House, circa 1919

What brought Page national fame, however, was his winning 100-word entry in a 1918 contest to write an American Creed. At a time when the United States was engaged in a world war and many of its citizens were first- or second-generation Americans, the contest was conceived of as a way to motivate citizens to stay loyal to their country.

Page explained that while walking home along Wisconsin Avenue after church service, he was inspired to write a creed along the lines of the Apostle's Creed that he had just recited. His entry, which was passed as a resolution by the House, read:

> I believe in the United States of America, as a government of the people, by the people, for the people; whose just powers are derived from the consent of the governed; a democracy in a republic; a sovereign Nation of many sovereign States; a perfect union, one and inseparable; established upon those principles of freedom, equality, justice, and humanity for which American patriots sacrificed their lives and fortunes.

> I therefore believe it is my duty to my country to love it, to support its Constitution, to obey its laws, to respect its flag, and to defend it against all enemies.

It is an inspirational summary, incorporating phrases from the Declaration of Independence, the preamble to the Constitution, Lincoln's Gettysburg Address, and Daniel Webster's reply to Robert Y. Hayne in the Senate in 1830 (regarded as the most famous oration in Senate history).

Unlike the Apostle's Creed, Pope's American Creed has not withstood the march of time. Indeed, I had never heard of it before undertaking this local historical exploration. But the concept of an American creed has endured since the beginning of the republic. In his landmark study of American racial attitudes and beliefs, Swedish economist Gunnar Myrdal wrote about the social and political ethos we hold in common, saying "this 'American Creed' is the cement in the structure of this great and disparate nation." Myrdal found that the African American population, though denied many of the benefits of the nation's high ideals, genuinely seemed to believe in the Creed in appealing their case for redress.

In 2018, former Secretary of State Condoleezza Rice and Pulitzer Prize-winning historian David M. Kennedy anchored a highly popular PBS documentary on what it means to be an American, entitled *American Creed*. Such a unifying theme is sorely needed today.

David M. Kennedy and Condoleezza Rice (Citizen Film & WTTW — Chicago Public Media/Sophie Constantinou)

Map — Tenleytown

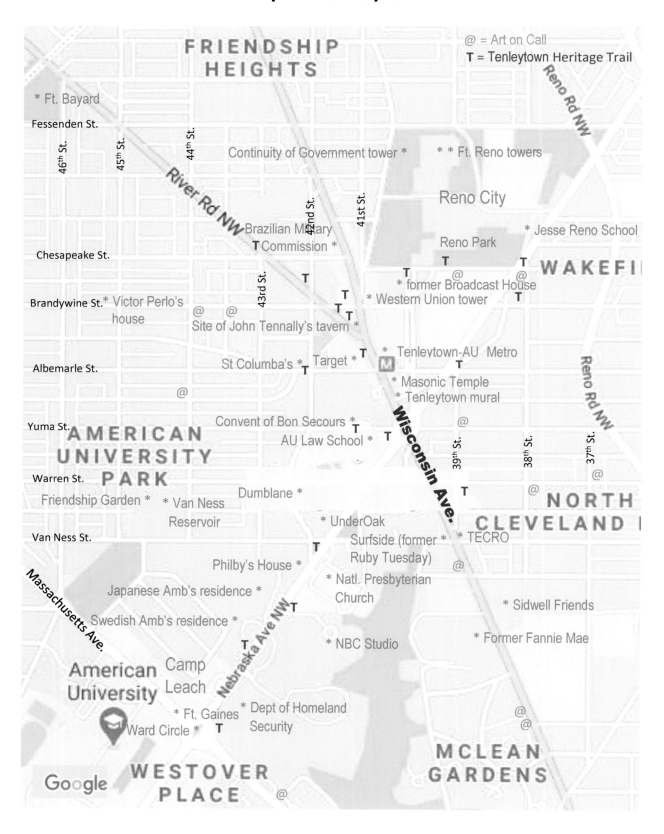

Part II: University Campus

19.   American University

With 14,000 students and covering 84 acres on three sides of Ward Circle, American University is the dominant institution in our neighborhood. Founded by Methodists, American University has maintained a close connection to the US government, hosting military units during both world wars and training prospective civil servants year-in and year-out.

American University president's office

eagle mascot in front of Federal Hall

AU, as it is commonly called, was chartered by an Act of Congress in 1893 at the urging of Methodist bishop John Fletcher Hurst, who aimed to create an institution that would promote public service, internationalism, and pragmatic idealism. He chose a location on the rural periphery of Washington at the former site of Fort Gaines *(story 7)*. It took a decade of fundraising before AU broke ground in 1902 and another decade before it began instruction in 1914, although classes were soon interrupted by the Great War.

The president's office commands the high ground next to Massachusetts Avenue, formerly a settler's homestead with a good view of the Potomac. The house was called "Friendship," after the estate *(story 12)*.

Hurst sought to establish a national Methodist university. Although the days of mandatory chapel services are long gone, a legal affiliation with the Methodist church remains. It is not a coincidence that the National United Methodist Church *(right)*

sits across Nebraska Avenue from the main campus, and that the Wesley Theological Seminary is adjacent to the campus on Massachusetts Avenue. But the place of worship on the university itself is the non-denominational Kay Spiritual Life Center *(below left)*, built in 1963. It is nicknamed the "flaming cupcake" due to its shape and 16-foot-tall impressionistic flame top.

From the beginning, and uncommon in higher education at the time, AU admitted women (before they could vote) and African Americans (when Washington was segregated). According to the university's website, it today draws students from all 50 states and well over 100 countries.

What is now the School of Public Affairs was founded in 1934 to educate future government employees in new approaches to public administration introduced by the New Deal. In a speech at its launch, President Franklin Roosevelt emphasized cooperation between the school and his administration.

In the late 1950s and early 1960s, the Department of Defense and the CIA operated the Special Operations Research Office as a think tank at American University under a counter-insurgency program focused on Latin America. The government abandoned the think tank after its research was criticized as imperialistic. Today, the university is known, *inter alia*, for the 1,145 graduates who have joined the Peace Corps.

American University quadrangle

20. 'Merican

In spring 2020, seeing a vandalized sign on a building on New Mexico Avenue at the eastern edge of American University brought a smile, reminding me of the meme of good old boys calling themselves "'Mericans." In thinking about it more, though, and talking about it with my wife Kyoko, we realized that even when the "A" is not purposely dropped, interlocutors often hear it that way because Americans accent the word's second syllable. The Chinese call our country *Měiguó* (美国), which it is. The characters mean "beautiful country," a name chosen both for its virtue and because the character for beauty is pronounced "*Měi*." In southern China, however, the Hokkien dialect transliterates "America" as "*Meilika*" (米利坚), the first syllable of which, 米, means "rice."

When wheat flour was introduced to Japan, it was called メリケン粉 (*meriken-ko*, "American powder"). Kyoko says using this word now can make one sound old-fashioned. In Vietnamese, a common word for America is *Mỹ*. In Swahili, it is *Marekani*. In Korean, *Miguk*. Speakers of these languages apparently did not hear the "A" in America.

So, what does all this have to do with American University? Well, a fifth of AU students come from foreign countries. At least some of them might have seen the vandalized sign (now fixed) as the appropriate pronunciation.

21.   Ward Circle

Washington, DC is chockablock with monuments and statues. Thirteen are in honor of George Washington. Contrary to what some Washingtonians think, one of these is not at Ward Circle. They might be forgiven for the mistake: from afar the statue does look a bit like the father of our country. It usually can only be seen from afar because there is no pedestrian access to the tree-enclosed figure at the center of the busy traffic circle.

A book published in 1921 by a like-named great-grandson characterized Artemas Ward as the first commander-in-chief of the American Revolution. The inscription at the base of his statue at Ward Circle calls him the "First Commander of the Patriot Forces." True. In 1775, as head of the Massachusetts militia, he had overall command of the Boston siege prior to Washington's arrival. In July that year, the Continental Congress appointed Washington as the first commander-in-chief of the Continental Army, and Ward as his second-in-command.

Ward Circle is surrounded on three sides by American University. Yet Ward has no connection to the university other than his surname on the School of Public Affairs building until the name was changed in 2017. An article for the University's Office of Campus Life a few years ago was cleverly headlined "Artemas Ward: AU's Second Cousin, Completely Removed."

So why is the statue there? In the 1920s, Ward's great-grandson donated $4 million to Harvard University, his alma mater, with the stipulation that a statue be erected honoring his ancestor. Harvard commissioned the statue and donated it to the US government after an architectural competition chose a design by Leonard Crunelle, which omitted the customary horse for Ward to mount. In 1938, the National Capital Park and Planning Commission deposited the 27-foot bronze at the intersection of Massachusetts and Nebraska Avenues, surrounded by a traffic circle.

22.   American University Law School

Up until the 20th century, it was commonly considered that "women did not have the mentality for law," as the law school of Columbian College (now George Washington University) told several female applicants. To offer opportunities in the legal profession, two pioneering women, Ellen Spencer Mussey and Emma Gillett, in 1896 founded a Woman's Law Class in downtown Washington.

The Washington College of Law, as it was incorporated in 1898, was the first law school to be founded by women, the first with a female dean, and the first to graduate an all-female class. It soon became co-educational. The WCL merged with American University (AU) in 1949 and graduated its first African American student in 1953. For thirty years the school was housed on the AU main campus, but expanded enrollment required a move in 1996 to larger premises a half-mile away next to the Spring Valley Shopping Center. Later, in 2016, the law school moved to its current eight-acre location on Tenley Circle.

The campus added two new buildings to an existing structure that formerly housed Immaculata Seminary, an all-girls primary, secondary, and postsecondary school run by the Catholic Sisters of Providence of Saint Mary-of-the-Woods. Immaculata closed in 1978 due to financial difficulties and the sisters sold the building to American University. Most structures on the site were torn down, but the Immaculata building remains as a protected landmark under DC law.

Immaculata Seminary, 1930
(Washington Board of Trade)

The Tenleytown history book previously cited says: "In 1905, when the new Immaculata school was completed and electrically lighted at night for the first time, streetcars and automobiles stopped for their occupants to see the amazing sight on top of Mount Marian, as the Immaculata hill was called."

On the ground behind the college, the old elementary school is also a protected landmark. This was the original Dumblane house discussed in story 5.

23. John F. Kennedy Speech Plaza

While exploring American University campus the first time, I was delighted to happen across a plaque commemorating President John F. Kennedy's June 10, 1963 commencement address. He dedicated the speech to "the most important topic on earth: world peace," and used it to advocate a treaty to ban atmospheric nuclear tests. The plaque, and the plaza from which Kennedy spoke, is on a knoll on the south side of the main athletic field.

(John F. Kennedy Presidential Library and Museum)

It had been nine years since Indian President Jawaharlal Nehru had first called for a halt to nuclear testing. Concerned about radioactive fallout, many global citizens wanted a comprehensive ban on testing nuclear weapons. But the dominant view among US officials was that a prohibition on underground tests could not be adequately verified. Instead, the United States, Soviet Union, and United Kingdom, the three main nuclear powers at the time, negotiated what was called a "Treaty Banning Nuclear Weapon Tests in the Atmosphere, in Outer Space and Under Water," also known as the Partial Test Ban Treaty (PTBT) or Limited Test Ban Treaty. It was signed on August 5, 1963 and ratified by the US Senate just 50 days later by a vote of 80–14. Imagine that! Such speed, sensibility, and bipartisanship.

Up to then, the United States had conducted 216 atmospheric, underwater, and space tests. The last one was on October 30, 1962, at Johnson Atoll in the Pacific Ocean. The Soviet Union had carried out almost the same number, 219, while the United Kingdom had tested 21 times, mostly in Australia. France and China did not join the PTBT and continued atmospheric testing, France until 1974 and China until 1980. French tests were conducted in Algeria and French Polynesia.

Meanwhile, underground nuclear testing continued to be carried out by the original five nuclear powers, later joined by India, Pakistan, North Korea, and probably Israel (it is not 100% proven that Israel and South Africa jointly tested a nuclear weapon in the southern Indian Ocean in 1979, as many experts believe). To date, there have been over 2,000 confirmed nuclear tests, more than half of them by the United States.

Negotiations over testing took many more years, but in 1996 finally produced the Comprehensive Test Ban Treaty (CTBT). By then, the science of seismology had advanced to the point that it was almost impossible to mask any underground test that would be of military significance. Since cheating could be detected, concerns about inadequate verification lost their salience. Experts also rebutted arguments that testing was needed in order to keep US weapons safe and reliable; computers are more accurate at checking weapon reliability. However, many skeptical politicians continued to contend otherwise. When the Republican-led Senate first blocked debate on the treaty, then quickly forced a ratification vote in October 1999, it was rejected by a vote of 51 to 48, far short of the two-thirds necessary for ratification. Despite overwhelming public support for ending nuclear testing, efforts over the past two decades to build Senate support for ratification have continued to be stymied by an anti-arms control mentality. Opponents want to keep an option to test again, even though this would mean other countries also keeping that option and undermining US credibility in opposing North Korea's nuclear testing.

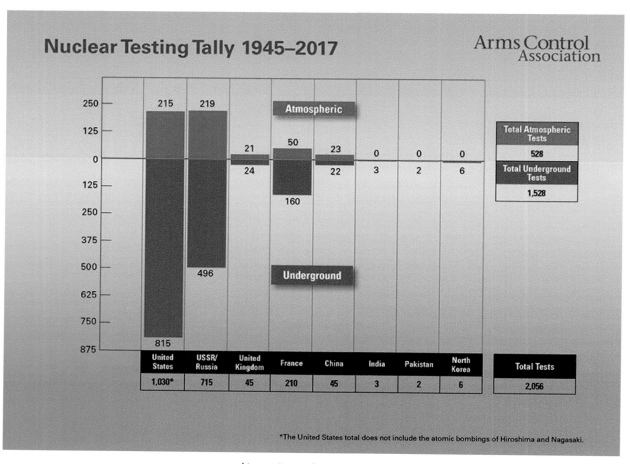

(Arms Control Association)

24. Easter Island Statue

In an alcove on the north side of the American University campus between Hughes and McDowell Halls stands a nine-foot, 8,000-pound Easter Island *moai* (statue). Between the years 1400 and 1600, the Rapa Nui people carved about 900 such monolithic figures, which represent deified ancestors. Many of them were set up on platforms around the island's perimeter, facing inwards, as if to watch over the people. The largest *moai* were more than 32 feet high and weighed over 80 tons. The average is about 13 feet, making the replica at American University small by comparison. It was carved from volcanic rock from Easter Island by Rapa Nui artisans for a 1999 exhibit at the American Museum of Natural History in New York City. In presenting the *moai* in 2000, the newly arrived Chilean ambassador noted American University's study-abroad programs in Chile. He also referred to the many nations that are represented on campus. The dean of the AU law school was from Chile and several other AU faculty members have longstanding ties to the country.

Easter Island has belonged to Chile since 1888. That year, the Chilean government purchased it from Alexander Salmon, a British-Tahitian merchant who had managed to buy up all the land on the island. Salmon did not have to complete all that many sales, because at the time the island population was not much more than 100, compared to an estimated 3,000 in 1770. The land had been depopulated due to deforestation, Peruvian slave raiders, and Western diseases. Easter Island is over 2,000 miles (3,500 kilometers) away from continental Chile. Other than being the closest continental state, if you call 2,000 miles close, Chile had no previous connection to Easter Island. But the 19th century was the age of acquisition and Chile wanted to play the game. The Indigenous people call the island Rapa Nui. It acquired its Western name from Dutch explorer Jacob Roggeveen who, on Easter Sunday (April 5) 1722, was the first European to visit the island.

Chile has other connections to American University. Orlando Letelier, who was assassinated in Washington in 1976 by agents of the Pinochet regime, had been serving on the faculty of the AU School of International Service. In 2016, Chilean President Michelle Bachelet visited the university to dedicate a mural by Letelier's son, Francisco.

25.   Korean Stone Grandfathers

Almost everywhere else in the world, the paired guardians of temples, halls, and other public places are fearsome in appearance: stone lions, chiseled dragons, carved warriors, and the like. In South Korea's southern island of Jeju (or Cheju, as it used to be romanized), the guardians are instead humorous-looking grandfathers. A decade ago, four of these *dolhareubang* (stone grandfathers) found their way to American University, where they stand guard in pairs over pleasant spots on the campus next to the School of International Service.

Kyoko and Mark Fitzpatrick in Jeju, May 1981

Seeing them reminded me of the fun visit Kyoko and I made to Jeju in 1981, when I was stationed in South Korea on my first assignment as a US diplomat. We enjoyed a wonderful two years there, greatly enhanced by the six months' language training we received beforehand. We were not fully fluent, but we could converse and Koreans were happy that we made the effort.

It was delightful to realize how similar the Korean language is to Japanese. Although mutually incomprehensible and using different common scripts, they share the same syntax and the same borrowed Chinese words and characters. The similarity is said to be akin to the closeness of English and Russian, with their common roots in Greek and Roman.

In 2011, the provincial government of Jeju and the South Korean Embassy also gave American University a set of *jeongnang* gate pillars and several plants to complement a Korean garden. It features three Korean cherry trees that Rhee Syng-man, who was to become South Korea's first president, planted there in 1943. He was invited by then-university president Paul Douglass, who had worked as a missionary in Korea. The trees represented Korean hopes for independence.

An article in the Korean press at the time of the garden opening quoted the dean of the School of International Service saying: "An environmentally friendly Korean garden with Rhee Syng-man cherry blossoms will rectify the wrong perception of Americans that all cherry trees are from Japan."

In 2003, the entire campus of American University was designated as an arboretum. In addition to cherry trees, the campus features magnolias, dogwoods, redbuds, and gingko, as well as many kinds of perennials and ornamental grasses. The quad features a magnificent scarlet oak, which is DC's state tree (if only DC were a state!).

(Jeff Watts, "Korean Garden," American University)

Jeongnang gate pillar

scarlet oak on the quad

26. Katzen Arts Center

The structural gem of American University is the relatively new art building at the northwest corner of Ward Circle, where Fort Gaines and Camp Leach once stood. Opened in 2005, the Cyrus and Myrtle Katzen Arts Center resulted from a $15 million gift by a former dentist turned real estate magnate and his artistic wife. Cyrus Katzen was an early pioneer in developing the business hubs of Baileys Crossroads, Tysons Corner, and Crystal City.

In addition to providing the seed money for the center and $5 million worth of art from his and Myrtle's own collection, Cyrus Katzen persuaded the city to grant a zoning license. When the university had earlier tried to build a new law school there, neighbors had strongly objected. When repeated hearings before the DC Zoning Commission also turned down the application for an arts center, Katzen arranged a meeting with Mayor Anthony Williams and feigned offering his money to George Mason University in Fairfax County, Virginia, instead. That got the mayor's support, which helped change the zoning commission's decision.

The center is home to all of the university's visual and performing arts programs, housed in the three-story American University Museum and adjoining sculpture garden. The 130,000-square-foot museum showcases pieces by Pablo Picasso, Marc Chagall, Willem de Kooning, and Roy Lichtenstein, all gifts from the Katzens. The museum also includes art by Jean Dubuffet, Amedeo Modigliani, Frank Stella, and Andy Warhol. Rotating exhibits feature contemporary art from the nation's capital region and from around the world. Recent additions include 9,000 pieces from the Corcoran Gallery of Art, which was dissolved in 2014. A new program, called the Alper Initiative dedicates research and display space for the art history of the capital. The building is also rented out for weddings.

Cyrus' personal history has an interesting twist. At age 16, his application to be a messenger boy for the FBI was rejected. Decades later, when he was able to retrieve his file under the Freedom of Information Act, it included just his 1935 job application with an attached memo from Clyde Tolson, deputy to bureau director J. Edgar Hoover, saying that Katzen was turned down because of his "foreign appearance" (he was Jewish) and because "he will not develop."

27.   WWI Camps

When the United States entered the first world war, the president of American University granted the government 92 acres of its sprawling and still little-used campus for whatever purpose desired. Gladly taking up the offer, the government stationed thousands of army recruits at the university for training before sending them across the Atlantic to fight in Europe. It was the site of the largest military encampment within the DC borders.

The area of the campus to the south and west was named American University Experimental Station (a.k.a. Camp AU) and was the site of chemical weapons testing, as explored in story 29. The area north of Massachusetts Avenue was called Camp Leach, home, *inter alia*, to advanced research, development, and testing of modern camouflage techniques. The soldiers transformed the area into practice battlefields. In both places, hundreds of barracks and training buildings were erected. Five bungalows for Army officers and their families were built on 44th Street.

Camp Leach seen from Hurst Hall looking northward. (American University Archives and Special Collections)

"Lumberjack Regiment" on AU parade ground, with residential houses in background (US National Archives)

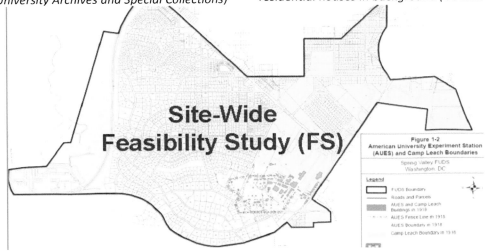

The yellow area was the boundary of Fort Leach and training grounds. Blue depicts the American University Experimental Station. (US Army Corps of Engineers)

According to Judith Beck Helm, "The citizens of Tenleytown were generous in their personal welcomes to the soldiers." Many families invited soldiers to dinner and made rooms available to soldiers' families and girlfriends so they could say goodbye before the young men were shipped off. The Singleton Masonic Lodge drew such large attendance that its Grand Visitations were shifted to a lecture hall at the university. Local churches set up special services and bible classes at the camps and took turns hosting Monday

training at Camp AU (US Army Corps of Engineers)

night socials. When the influenza pandemic hit in 1918, however, the church services had to be curtailed, along with school classes. I have not come across any reports of protests claiming that civil liberties were violated by these closings (in contrast to current times). All was not sweetness and light, however, as German-American citizens of Tenleytown suffered from discrimination. One German immigrant was removed from his post at the Reno reservoir, for fear he might poison the water.

Uniformed personnel returned to American University in 1945 when it hosted the US Navy Bomb Disposal School on five acres abutting the Music Conservatory on the west side of the campus. In addition to ten buildings it initially occupied, the Navy built 18 more there.

Live bombs were prohibited on the university compound, so trainees practiced disposal techniques on simulated bombs that had small amounts of fulminate of mercury to produce a "bang." However, one day an instructor, in violation of policy, brought a live 50-millimeter shell onto school grounds and fired it into or over the adjacent neighborhood. I trust it was recovered and removed.

*training at the US Navy Bomb Disposal School
(American University Archives
and Special Collections)*

28. Chemical Weapons Program

A plaque on the McKinley Building, one of the first structures on the AU campus and now home to the School of Communications, boasts of it being the birthplace of the Army Chemical Corps. As noted in story 27, when the United States joined the fight against the Axis Powers in 1917, the board of trustees of the new American University offered the government use of the campus to support the war effort in whatever way desired. In addition to training troops, the government decided to use it for chemical warfare laboratories and proving grounds. In other words, chemical weapons were developed and tested here.

 The US Army Corps of Engineers established Camp Leach and the newly created Gas Service on the campus. Meanwhile, the Department of Interior Bureau of Mines founded the American University Experiment Station (also called Camp AU). Utilizing over 150 buildings with close to 2,000 personnel, the program outfitted the campus and surrounding land with underground concrete pits, trenches, and open ranges for field tests of chemical weapons utilizing mustard gas, lewisite, ricin, cyanogen, chloride, phosgene, chlorine and cyanide. More about that in the next story.

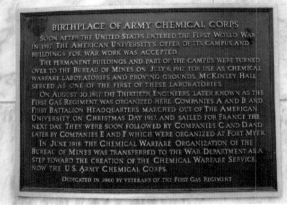

plaque on McKinley Building (left)

30th Engineers Receiving Training in Trench Warfare.
Inscribed on back: " 'Hell fire' or Gas and Flame Regiment became 1st Gas Regiment of newly created Chemical Warfare Service in July 1918." (American University Archives and Special Collections)

29. Death Valley

Just west of American University is an upscale quiet residential development with large houses, well-kept yards, mature shade trees and curvy roads. It is a lovely place to stroll. During new home construction in the 1990s, however, it was discovered that beauty is only skin deep. The ground was contaminated because the area had been America's principal testing station for development of poisonous gases and chemical munitions for use in WWI, under the Army program at AU *(previous story)*.

Stray dogs, goats and other animals were tied to stakes while soldiers set off chemical bombs and watched the animals agonizingly die. Soldiers called the area Death Valley. After the war, the Army returned the university's land and sold the adjoining farmland, where munitions had been tested and dumped, to the Miller Development Company to build this fancy neighborhood. Death Valley became the prestigious DC bedroom community of Spring Valley.

(National Archives)

Field Kennel, Chemical Warfare Service (National Archives)

In 1993, workers constructing new houses in Spring Valley uncovered rusted cannisters. Army bomb-removal units determined that they were WWI-era chemical mortar rounds and 75-millimeter shells. Some were live and might contain lethal mustard gas. Over the next year, under Operation Safe Removal, the Army Corps of Engineers recovered 141 munitions from Spring Valley, including 42 poison-gas shells. In stages, officials evacuated 72 homes in the zone around the bomb pit and searched for buried munitions. It was the only residential area designated under the Army's formerly used defense sites (FUDS) environmental restoration program.

outside Hamilton Hall, September 2007 (Allen Hengst)

In 1995, the Army issued a report saying it had completed its work and that Spring Valley was safe. "No further action" was required. The president of the Miller Development Company said "we could market this as the safest area in the world after the careful scrutiny of the Army." But an environmental specialist for the DC health department found discrepancies in the report and inadequate testing for arsenic. Then in 1996, landscapers planting a tree in front of the AU president's home at 4835 Glenbrook Road unearthed broken bottles emitting fumes that burned their eyes. A test found levels of arsenic in the soil 28 times above what the government considers acceptable.

Prodded by the district health department, the Army Corps of Engineers returned to Spring Valley to reanalyze the coordinates for a large burial pit that was depicted in an eerie photograph from 1918. The image shows a soldier wearing a gas mask on a hillside covered with bare trees next to a trench and a jumble of five-gallon jugs. Sergeant C.W. Maurer had inscribed on the back: "The Pit, the most feared and respected place in the grounds. The bottles are full of mustard, to be destroyed here, in Death Valley, the hole called Hades."

"The Hole called Hades," front and back (courtesy of the estate of Addie Ruth Maurer Olson)

Using more exact mapping and photographic analysis techniques than in previous investigations, the search for a "hole called Hades" led the Army Corps of Engineers to the South Korean ambassador's residence garden and to the property next door at 4825 Glenbrook Road. Over 680 items associated with chemical munitions were eventually found. The mansion that once stood there was demolished in 2012. A large aluminum-plated structure, built to withstand munitions blasts and to contain and filter poisonous vapors, was installed at the site, as workers donned hazmat suits and breathing equipment. By summer 2020, the structure was mostly removed.

The wartime use of chemical and biological weapons was banned by the 1925 Geneva Protocol. But the weapons themselves were not prohibited until the 1993 Chemical Weapons Convention. The convention is close to being universally accepted, with only Egypt, North Korea and South Sudan not having signed and Israel having signed but not yet ratified. However, recent use of chemical weapons by Syria, under Russia's diplomatic protection, has severely undermined the international norm against chemical weapons.

50

Map — American University, Spring Valley

Light gray contour depicts informal boundaries of Spring Valley

Part III: The Past Century

30. Spring Valley

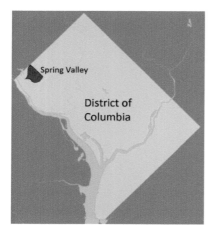

District of Columbia

As discussed in the previous story, the land that soldiers had nicknamed "Death Valley" in 1918 became the prestigious DC bedroom community of Spring Valley in the 1930s. Lyndon Johnson and Richard Nixon both lived in Spring Valley before they became president. Tycoon Warren Buffett lived there as a teenager when his father was a congressman from Nebraska. Buffett attended public schools in Tenleytown and made money by installing pinball machines in local barbershops. The area is still home to the rich and famous.

So, I should be excited to share the same zip code. But in addition to the World War I–era chemical weapons that were simply bulldozed over, Spring Valley has another dark history. Not so long ago, the neighborhood restricted homeownership on the basis of race. In 1929, the Miller Development Company promoted Spring Valley as "safe from the invasion of the changing character of [Washington, DC] neighborhoods." White flight from DC's inner city was beginning and Spring Valley was a refuge for upper-middle-class WASPs.

4211 49th St., where Warren Buffett lived as a teenager

Buyers had to sign restrictive covenants that prohibited home sales to African Americans and those of "the Semitic race... [including] Armenians, Jews, Hebrews, Persians, and Syrians." Richard Nixon signed such a covenant in 1952 when, as vice president, he bought a $41,000 home at 4801 Tilden Street. Such restrictive covenants were held unconstitutional by the Supreme Court in 1940.

Today, Spring Valley residents include former Attorney General Eric Holder and Washington Nationals co-owners Ed and Debra Cohen. It is

4801 Tilden St., home of Richard Nixon as vice president

still very white, however. And being far from the Metro, it remains economically exclusive.

According to a thesis on Washington, DC land use, the discovery of buried munitions and elevated levels of arsenic had little effect on home values. In 1990, prior to the chemical weapons discovery, the median home value for Spring Valley was $1.01 million (adjusted to 2020 dollars); in 2000, the median home value was $1.04 million (adjusted to 2020 dollars). Today it is $1.8 million. The market value for Nixon's former house is considerably below this, at $1.3 million.

It is curious that Nixon's house was not set off from the sidewalk. Lyndon Johnson's estate at 52nd Street allowed for more protection. He and his wife had purchased it in 1961 from socialite Perle Mesta, who grandly dubbed it "Les Ormes." The Johnsons paid about $160,000 for the mansion and anglicized its name to The Elms. "Every time somebody calls it a château, I lose 50,000 votes back in Texas," Johnson sighed. Today, it is the residence of the ambassador of Algeria.

4040 52nd St., now Algerian ambassador's residence

The Elms when it was home to Lyndon B. Johnson (Library of Congress)

It was good that The Elms had fences and space for a guard house, because it served as the presidential office for several weeks at the end of 1963 while Jackie Kennedy arranged to move out of the White House after her husband's assassination. The fatal attack on President Kennedy triggered legislation in 1966 to provide for an official residence for the vice president. Until it was decided in 1974 to use the Chief of Naval Operation's house at Naval Observatory Circle for that purpose, the Secret Service paid for expensive upgrades to the private homes of vice presidents Hubert Humphrey, Spiro Agnew, and Gerald Ford. Agnew lived in his house for only three months in 1973 before resigning; shortly thereafter, he sold it at a large profit, in part because of the government-funded upgrades.

Another Spring Valley resident was senior Soviet diplomat Arkady Shevchenko, who defected to the United States in 1978 when he was a United Nations undersecretary general, a move that stunned the international diplomatic community. He later married an American woman and lived with her at 4941 Tilden Street.

31.   Convent of Bon Secours

During the Roaring Twenties, when socialite Evalyn Walsh McLean flaunted her wealth at the Friendship estate *(story 17)*, a group of women a few blocks to the north showed a different face of humanity. In 1928, the Convent of Bon Secours ("good help") opened at 4101 Yuma Street, just off Wisconsin Avenue. The good sisters worked as nurses, caring for both wealthy and needy patients. They were particularly appreciated during typhoid and influenza epidemics.

Washington convent, 1961 (Sisters of Bon Secours USA Archives)

The order originated in France in 1824, with the mission of caring for patients from all socio-economic groups. They tended the wounded during the 1848 revolution in France and the 1870 Franco-Prussian War. In 1881, the order expanded to America, opening a hospital in Baltimore. In 1907, the Sisters of Bon Secours in Baltimore provided the world's first recorded formal home health care service as well as the first day care facility, in order to help working mothers whose only alternative was to place their children in orphanages. The order added many more hospitals, as well as community health clinics, nursing care facilities, alcohol and drug abuse rehabilitation centers, and convalescent homes.

former convent at 4101 Yuma St.

After World War II, Americans increasingly turned to hospitals for nursing care. So, in the early 1960s, the sisters closed the convent on Yuma Street and sold the buff brick building to Rochambeau the French International School, which held classes there until 1975. The Oakcrest School, for Catholic girls, then took over the school until it relocated to Vienna, Virginia. In 2010, the Yuma Study Center, a DC women's leadership organization, established itself in the old convent, maintaining its gender identity.

32.   UnderOak

What was behind the fence?

I often wondered what was beyond the fence surrounding the three-acre property at 4220 Nebraska Avenue. All that was visible, on the south side facing Van Ness Street, was the top of a green copper turret of some sort. When my local history project gave me the impetus to investigate, I learned about the VIPs who lived in the house and about the origin of the "turret."

The Old English-style house there was built in 1924 by Scott E. Welker, who had made his fortune in the distilling business. The property was split off from the Dumblane estate to the north *(story 5)* and included a centuries-old white oak tree. As described by the May 1924 issue of *American Architect,* the house, named "Under-Oak," was built around "Washington's most magnificent huge oak."

In 1941, the estate was sold to Wiley and Ruth Buchanan. She was heiress to the founder of Dow Chemical; he was a government official. Under President Dwight Eisenhower, Wiley was ambassador to Luxembourg from 1953–1957 and then US Chief of Protocol. Later, in 1975 under President Gerald Ford, he was appointed ambassador to Austria. As Chief of Protocol, Buchanan dealt with many foreign leaders. According to his daughter Bonnie, once when the Buchanans were in a car with Nikita Khrushchev, the Soviet premier put his arm

Mrs. Wiley T. Buchanan shows her pool to Mrs. Khrushchev and her daughter Julia, Sept 26, 1959 (UPI)

Dede and Bonnie Buchanan, with oak tree on right, circa 1947 (courtesy of Bonnie Matheson)

around Wiley and said, using English (which most people did not know he spoke), "you think your capitalism is good, but your grandchildren will grow up to be communists." In fact, the opposite result transpired, as Khrushchev's grandchildren became capitalists.

While the Buchanans were in Luxembourg, they temporarily rented their house to Marjorie Merriweather Post, owner of General Foods, at one point the richest woman in America, and founder of the Mar-a-Lago mansion in Florida,

the famous oak cut back to its trunk

currently owned by Donald Trump. Later, while Wiley served in Vienna, UnderOak was rented to Henry Kissinger and his bride Nancy.

A 2012 article in *Washington Life* said the residence was one of the last privately owned estates in Washington. It also said that in addition to the venerable oak, the estate was noted for gardens designed in the 1950s by Rose Greely, the first licensed female landscape architect in Washington, DC. Unfortunately, in 2016 the dying oak tree had to be cut back to its trunk.

When Buchanan's daughter made her social debut, *Town & Country* magazine featured her on its June 1962 cover, calling her "Deb of the Year." Dede became a leading San Francisco socialite. Her stepson Sean Wilsey's gossipy memoir, *Oh the Glory of it All*, mentions Dede's second marriage, held at UnderOak in 1981.

Wiley Buchanan died from Alzheimer's disease in 1986 at age 72. Interestingly, his grandson, Trevor Traina, became ambassador to Austria in 2018 (as a political appointee). Ruth passed away at UnderOak in 2019, near the age of 102. The next year the property, valued at over $6.5 million, was put on the market. The part next to Van Ness Street, where the cupola stands, may be used for a school.

Ruth and grandson Amb. Trevor Traina, 2018 (used with his permission)

Crowdsourcing the question about the "turret" on Twitter produced interesting answers. Some followers guessed a dovecote, others an icehouse, a smokehouse, or a well. One sharp-eyed man thought the turret was probably a cupola salvaged from some older gutted structure. He was right. The cupola at one time stood atop a country house named Mount Alto in Glover Park, which became a school of domestic art and science and later a veteran's hospital. In 1967 when the building was to be torn down, Wiley Buchanan rescued its two cupolas and installed one on a brick base on his estate as a garden folly, which provided storage for lawnmowers and garden tools. The other he donated to the Washington Home hospice *(story 33)*. The Mount Alto site became home to the Russian Embassy *(story 57)*.

author with UnderOak cupola   *Washington Home cupola*

33. Sidwell Friends

What is arguably the most famous private school in DC is located just south of Tenleytown. Sidwell Friends is a Quaker co-ed day school founded by Thomas Sidwell in 1883. It started at a Quaker meeting house near the White House and moved in the 1920s to the then-suburban area at 3825 Wisconsin Avenue. The main administrative building, which Sidwell purchased in 1955, has a long history, dating to 1827 when it was built as the manor home for a large estate, "the Highlands." Allen Dulles lived there in 1953 when he became CIA director.

Sidwell Friends has 1,155 students, half of them students of color, although the first African American was not admitted until 1956. Tuition is not inexpensive: over $44,000 per year, similar to other private schools in the area, but 23% of students receive financial aid. Merit-based, Sidwell Friends accepts only 7% of applicants. An amusing blog by two DC moms in 2013 detailed the unsuccessful quests for their kids' admission.

Quaker beliefs and values continue to guide Sidwell Friends. Each week, all students and teachers meet together in shared silence: the Meeting for Worship, preceded with a question to contemplate. A fundamental Quaker belief is that there is "that of God" in everyone — that goodness and dignity are inherent in all human beings. The idea of conscience is paramount. One often hears the statement, "Let your life speak," which serves as a call to action, including on environmental stewardship. Both the Middle School and the Quaker Meeting House and Arts Center have the highest certification in "Leadership in Energy and Environmental Design."

Sidwell Friends Middle School, entrance on 37th St.

Consistent with the Quaker Testimony of Equality, the school does not rank its students. A snide article in the *Atlantic* in 2019 said Quaker schools have been able to retain many of their faith traditions despite welcoming a diverse student body because it is "the least oppressive religion on Earth." The article spoke about college counselors at the school being besieged by Ivy League-obsessed parents. It got so bad that the head of the school sent a letter to parents of high school seniors demanding that they stop "the verbal assault of employees."

A main factor in its fame is the student body, which has included Bill Nye The Science Guy and several children of sitting presidents, most recently, Malia and Sasha Obama. One reason the Obamas stayed in Washington after his presidency was so Sasha could continue her schooling there. She graduated in 2019, along with Joe and Jill Biden's granddaughter Maisy. When Chelsea Clinton graduated from the school in 1997, her father spoke at the graduation ceremony. Vice President Al Gore's son, Albert Gore III, also attended Sidwell Friends, as did President Nixon's daughter Tricia and, earlier, offspring of Herbert Hoover and Theodore Roosevelt. That all is a contrast to the decision by President Jimmy Carter and his wife Rosalynn to send their daughter Amy to a public DC school in 1977. She was the only child of a sitting president to attend a public school in the past century.

The law requiring Secret Service protection for immediate family of the president was reportedly only occasionally an issue. They tried to blend in by dressing like teachers. However, according to my cousin Kristin, whose boys attended Sidwell, the Secret Service agents clearly stuck out, in that they modeled themselves on a geeky teacher stereotype and had wires dangling from their ears.

Plans are underway for the Sidwell Friends Lower School, currently located 3.7 miles north in Bethesda, Maryland, to move to the main campus. This entailed purchase in 2016 of the adjacent Washington Home, a century-old nonprofit that provided nursing and hospice care to the elderly.

Chelsea Clinton with parents at her 1997 Sidwell high school graduation (White House photo)

The $32.5 million buy-out sparked protests over displacing the 100-plus seniors, many of whom were senile. For the "Harvard of Washington's private schools," controversy is part of the package.

(Forest Hills Connection)

34.   Van Ness Reservoir

A website called DC Urban Moms and Dads posed the question "What is buried in the AU Park block between Van Ness, Warren, and 44th St?" The first answer, from the general public was "I assume it's some military thing." Some of my neighbors have the same question-and-answer about the flat-topped low hill. One friend asked if it is some kind of secret intelligence post. The CCTV cameras at every corner, multiple warning signs, and high fence topped with barbed wire fan such suspicions.

The truth is much more prosaic. It is just an underground reservoir, essentially a grass-covered large concrete box full of 14.5 million gallons of water, one of several in the area. The water originally comes from the Potomac River at Great Falls. From there, it runs ten miles downhill through a pre-Civil War pipe running from the Potomac to the Dalecarlia Water Treatment Plant a mile and a half away. After being filtered, disinfected, and fluoridated, the water is pumped up to the reservoirs and water towers on the highest elevations in the district, from where it flows via gravity to the rest of the city. The water stays in the tanks for only three days at most.

Officially called the Second High Reservoir, the water tank at Van Ness is part of the Washington Aqueduct, one of the first water systems of its type in the United States. Portions of it entered service in 1859. The full pipeline began operating in 1864, though the Van Ness Reservoir and its connecting pipes came in the latter half of the 1920s. The tight security is because the city's water system is considered to be critical infrastructure.

35. Alban Towers

A once-prestigious luxury apartment building sits diagonally across the Massachusetts-Wisconsin intersection from the Washington National Cathedral, which it was designed to complement, with similar gothic revival architecture. Its name comes from a colonial home called Mount Alban that once stood where the cathedral was built. When Alban Towers opened in 1929 at six stories tall, it was the largest apartment building in Washington, DC.

With 216 units, Alban Towers once offered its residents 24-hour maid service, a public dining room, a beauty shop, a travel agency, a grocery store, and a lunch counter. The lobbies and hallways were richly ornamented with gothic and art deco elements. It was the Washington residence of 1944 and 1948 Republican Party presidential nominee Thomas Dewey and of former Secretary of State Edmund Muskie, among other prominent politicians. It had both apartments and hotel suites. The building housed the DC headquarters of presidential campaigns for John F. Kennedy,
Eugene McCarthy, Richard Nixon, and Ronald Reagan. During Kennedy's inauguration in 1961, Frank Sinatra, Bette Davis, and other prominent entertainers stayed at the building's upmarket hotel suites.

Many diplomats also stayed at Alban Towers over the years. A problem arose, however, when, after World War II, the embassies of newly independent African states attempted to lease some of its apartments. Washington was still racially segregated at the time and Alban Towers and other area apartment buildings refused residence to the African diplomats.

lobby and portico of Alban Towers

Perhaps the most famous diplomat resident was Tamon Yamaguchi, a sophisticated naval attaché in the mid-1930s who had attended Princeton University. He has been called a "Japanese James Bond." Attachés are officials, often possessing special expertise, who are "attached" to the diplomatic staff of an ambassador. For example, in my diplomatic career, I was twice a labor attaché and briefly a science attaché (to the amusement of family members familiar with my paucity of science study). Military attachés are uniformed officers with diplomatic duties. It is understood that overt intelligence gathering (within legal bounds) is among their responsibilities. US defense attachés, for example, are managed by the Defense Intelligence Agency. Yamaguchi's activities went beyond the legal, however, in

Adm. Tamon Yamaguchi

using Alban Towers as a place to tap into official radio frequencies. He also recruited agents.

One of his marks was a disgraced, deeply in debt, and dishonorably discharged naval officer named John Semer Farnsworth (codename "Agent K"). The US Office of Naval Intelligence put Yamaguchi's luxury apartment under surveillance and made a surreptitious entry in the guise of painters but found nothing incriminating. Yamaguchi was recalled to Japan in 1936 under normal rotation after two years and was promoted to rear admiral. He later helped Admiral Isoroku Yamamoto plan the attack on Pearl Harbor. Yamaguchi nobly perished in the Battle of Midway when he chose to go down with his ship. He is far more famous for those exploits than for his spying deeds, which are not even mentioned in his English Wikipedia entry.

Alban Towers declined in status in the 1970s and was sold to Georgetown University for student housing in a quarter of its units. In the 1980s and 1990s, the building fell into a state of serious disrepair and efforts to sell to a developer fell through. Finally, in 1999, a real estate company bought the building and undertook a $63 million restoration effort, preserving the original architectural elements.

grotesques on the portico columns of Alban Towers

36. The Westchester

The Westchester, at 4000 Cathedral Avenue, has been called "a faded grande dame evoking the gentility of a bygone Washington." In its heyday in the 1940s, the luxury apartment complex was Washington's most elegant address. At the beginning of World War II, it housed 12 senators and 31 congressmen, 14 judges, and any number of spies and diplomats, including the secretary of the Persian legation. Another former resident was Kermit Roosevelt, Jr., a CIA officer who masterminded the coup d'état that returned the shah of Iran to power in 1953. Senator Barry Goldwater used to live in the apartment around the corner from a unit now occupied by my friends Jim Zumwalt and Ann Kambara, who encouraged me to include the Westchester in my neighborhood narratives.

A 1947 *Washington Post* article about a water cut-off to the upper floors of the complex (yes, they ran a story about that) listed eight senators who lived at the Westchester, all Republican. The manager laughingly "guessed we don't have any Democratic senators here." There were no vacancies when Ambassador Mike Mansfield and his wife Maureen inquired when he returned in 1988 from his ambassadorial posting in Tokyo, so they had to settle for a less hoity-toity apartment building across the street.

The Westchester was built in 1929 on a former dairy farm, after the streetcar line that was installed on Wisconsin Avenue made the area more accessible. It was planned to be the largest apartment house south of New York City, with eight buildings designed around a spacious quadrangle. But the Great Depression forced a halt to construction after five buildings were erected. The Westchester became a co-op in 1954, with 550 units.

According to a more recent *Washington Post* article, it is "high-rise living, 1930s style," with valet service, a hair salon, barbershop, a market, and until not long ago, a gas pump. It was the last elite apartment complex in the city with its own restaurant, which finally closed in 2016 (although the building residents are actively seeking a new restaurant tenant). The architecture is art deco inspired and the Georgian gates and pillars were imported from an estate in England that had been destroyed in World War II.

circa 1933 photograph showing the original buildings (Thomas Airviews)

The buildings rise no higher than eight floors because of a 1910 law that limits DC buildings to a maximum height of 130 feet and, in the case of residential buildings, eight floors. The law was originally enacted for fire safety reasons, but it was kept for aesthetics. The height restrictions go back to when President George Washington, who never actually governed from the city named after him, first ordered that the new capital city have a height limit at 40 feet. Common wisdom has it that the height of the Capitol's dome set the later limit, but that is not actually the case. The 130-foot figure was borrowed from Boston and Chicago's safety-oriented limits at the time.

Westchester main lobby and OB lobby (Jim Zumwalt)

Thanks to the city's height restrictions, the top floors of the Westchester have magnificent views. Oddly, however, the condo fees are reduced for the top two floors. According to Jim, this is because when the fee structure was set, those floors were more uncomfortable in summer, and even though modern air conditioning makes that irrelevant, the precedent was not changed.

In story 68, we will meet a Westchester couple who betrayed their country.

37. Wagshal's Deli

At a time when Spring Valley excluded Jews *(story 29)*, a Jewish delicatessen across the street from the community's northeast border became highly popular with its residents. As son Tom pointed out when I posted this story on Facebook, it has been a common practice for our society to ban membership of a group while simultaneously enjoying the benefits of that group's cuisine and culture. Mexican and other Latin American food, Southern Black soul food, and Jewish delis are all part of the pattern.

Wagshal's Deli was started in 1925 at 9th Street and G Street NW. Two years later, the deli moved to Adams Morgan, then in 1939 to the Spring Valley Shopping Center, at 4855 Massachusetts Avenue. It holds the oldest liquor license in the District of Columbia; when prohibition ended in 1933, founder Sam Wagshal was the first in line at the license office.

Wagshal's has been called "the president's deli," because Harry Truman, George H.W. Bush, Richard Nixon, Gerald Ford, and Bill Clinton have been among its loyal patrons. The business was often asked to cater White House-related events, including a big birthday party in 1956 for Nixon at the National Press Club.

Papa Bush endeared himself by taking his own place in the often-long lines at the checkout counter. He said waiting in line was part of the charm of the place. One of Bush's visits to the deli put him on the wrong side of the law. In 1981, the DC Alcoholic Beverage Control Board launched an investigation into a report that the deli illegally sold liquor on credit to the incoming vice president a week before his inauguration. According to muckraking columnist Jack Anderson, Bush bought $77.72 in merchandise on credit, including Scotch whisky, rum, and vodka, asking that the bill be sent to the White House.

In 1990, the Wagshal family sold the operation, which has separate sites at the Spring Valley Shopping Center for its deli and its market. The shopping center itself was designated as a DC Historic Site in 1989.

38.   The Washington Ballet

Becoming a national treasure isn't easy. And just willing it so won't necessarily make it happen.

In 2014, The Washington Ballet, at 3515 Wisconsin Avenue, created a ten-year strategic plan with the goal of being among the top ballet companies in the nation by 2023. Aiming for those heights strained the nonprofit company's resources, however. In 2016, a new artistic director was hired at a 40% higher salary and given rent-free housing. The new artistic director, Julie Kent, native to the DC area, was a celebrated ballerina but new to management. Her understandable insistence on the company performing only to live music raised costs. She changed the programming from the playful repertoire of her predecessor to one focused more on the classics, which at the beginning at least, found less appeal to Washington audiences. Empty seats became common. Four popular dancers left in 2018. By that autumn, the company was $3 million in the hole.

The company dates to 1944, when Mary Day established The Washington School of Ballet. In 1976, she started The Washington Ballet as a showcase for her trainees. In 1999, new Artistic Director Septime Webre broadened the company's scope, including by initiating a partnership with the DC public school system called DanceDC. The following year, he led The Washington Ballet on a tour of Havana, making it the first US ballet company to perform in Cuba since 1960. When Webre left, the board of directors hired Kent as part of its plan to reinvent The Washington Ballet as a bigger, better company.

Former interim executive director, Shakira Segundo told the *Washington Post* in 2018 that in the Webre years, most audience members "were not ballet fans. They were the general public who came to see a show. … Now they're throwing them into the deep end, saying, 'Love it.' " Kent's response to the *Post* was to ask for patience because it takes time to "build something great."

In July 2020, however, the company was still seeking its footing. Three executive directors left since Kent became artistic director. And like all other performing arts companies in the United States, The Washington Ballet had to postpone all live performances through 2020 due to the coronavirus. It is a shame that classes also had to be cancelled. The school, which operates at three locations on Wisconsin Avenue, has greatly benefited the community.

39. Victory Garden

The community garden on the west side of the Van Ness Reservoir started off in WWII as one of the victory gardens that the government encouraged as a way to reduce pressure on the public food supply and as a civil morale booster. The name today is Friendship Garden, because it is associated with the Friendship Recreation Center (a.k.a. Turtle Park), directly to the south. My guess is that because of its close proximity to the reservoir built in the late 1920s, the land, apparently used for farming, remained undeveloped while tract housing was subsequently built on surrounding blocks in the following years.

After victory in 1945, the victory garden went away, to be revived in the late 1960s by a group of what local historians call hippies. When they moved on in life, the community garden became more formalized and was registered with the city. It is one of 26 community gardens in the district, part of a green gentrification movement. Most of the gardeners at Friendship Garden live close by, but some come from as far as two miles away.

Friendship Garden (with Gideon in foreground)

Initially, Friendship Garden did not have a water supply, even though it was right next to 14.5 million gallons of H_2O. People had to haul water for their plants in jugs from their houses. A pipe and faucets were installed in about 1980 in fulfillment of an election pledge by then-mayor Marion Barry. (Barry was a civil rights activist and worthy politician who, sadly, is best remembered nationally for his 1990 cocaine bust and the remark, "The bitch set me up.")

One of the longtime gardeners said that in the past they did not to have to worry about deer and rabbits. Both are now frequent visitors, so all the plots have to be protected with critter-proof high fences. In the early days, most plots were about 500 square feet, but many became subdivided, as interest in communal gardening grew. Today some are as small as 135 square feet. There is a waiting list of two to four years to get one of the 50 plots. Assigned spaces are distributed when people opt out, die, or their plants die for lack of maintenance. Among the other rules is that all fertilizers or sprays must be organic.

40.   Western Union Tower

After World War II, the Western Union Telegraph Company embarked on an experiment to replace century-old wire telegraphy with microwave transmission technology developed during the war. A 73-foot limestone tower built at 4623 41st Street, just off Wisconsin Avenue south of Fort Reno, was part of this effort. As mentioned, this area is the highest elevation in the city.

It was the southernmost of 25 towers erected between New York City, Pittsburgh, and Washington. The Washington tower is America's only architect-designed building built solely as an antenna structure. It was created by architect Leon Chatelain, a mason, in art deco style.

This new technology helped erase telegraph wires and poles from the landscape. In addition, the tower was designed to relay recently invented television signals, which gave Western Union and its partner RCA a head start in the television revolution of the 1950s. During the Cold War era, the tower also handled national security communications. In 1996, it became a cellular telephone transmitter.

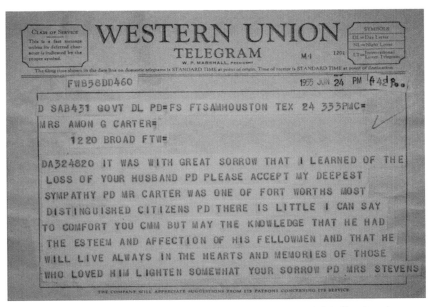

(The University of Texas at Arlington Library Special Collections)

41. Gandhi and Monism

Among the nearly 20 houses of worship in our neighborhood, one is different in nearly every way — beliefs, architecture, history — from most of the others. The Golden Lotus Temple at 4748 Western Avenue, Bethesda, just across the DC border, was completed in 1952 for the Self-Revelation Church of Absolute Monism. The founder was Swami Premananda, who was recruited from India in 1928 to lead the congregation. In 1959, he also established the Mahatma Gandhi Memorial Foundation which later built the Gandhi Memorial Center. A blue reflecting pool in front of the temple is built in the shape of a left foot, representing "the lasting imprint left by great souls."

Srimati Karuna next to Gandhi statue

The purpose of the foundation is to "disseminate and represent the philosophy, ideal, life, service, and teachings of Mahatma Gandhi, as well as the cultural heritage of India." At a time when Gandhi is "falling out of sync with the prevailing trends in Indian politics," to quote the *New York Times*, I am happy to see his example of nonviolent resistance promoted. His teachings are a useful antidote to the extreme Hindu nationalism that is prevalent in India today.

"Absolute Monism," referring to the ancient Hindu philosophy called Advaita Vedanta, dating back many centuries BCE, is the paradigmatic example of Hindu spirituality. Monism (derived from the Greek *monos* meaning "single" and "without division") is the theological view that all is one. According to the church website, "Absolute Monism originated in the divine consciousness of the soul of man." A philosophy website sums up Absolute Monism as meaning "there is only one substance and only one being." A recent bestseller about 19th-century German polymath Alexander Von Humboldt called monism "the most important *ersatz* religion at the turn of the twentieth century." The philosophy is taught through the science of Yoga and meditation.

Interesting facts: Swami Premananda was a 33rd degree Freemason. For most of the past 45 years, the church and foundation were headed by Swami Kamalananda, whose female gender bucked tradition. Her successor as director of the center and full-time minister of the church, Srimati Karuna, is also female. The library at the center features a bronze life-size statue of Gandhi, created by British sculptor Clara Quien in 1946–47.

42.   Washington Hebrew Congregation

The largest Jewish congregation in the DC metropolitan area and one of the largest Reform congregations in the world has its temple in the southwest corner of the McLean Gardens, at 3935 Macomb Street NW.

The Washington Hebrew Congregation (WHC) became the first Jewish assembly in Washington, DC in 1852 when 21 German-speaking immigrants met in a home on Pennsylvania Avenue. Four years later, they successfully persuaded Congress to pass an act that conferred all the "rights, privileges, and immunities heretofore granted by law to the Christian churches… to the Hebrew congregation." In 1863, they converted a church at 8th Street and I Street NW as WHC's first permanent home. A schism soon developed, however, over religious reforms, including the use of German and English during services. The introduction of a musical organ in 1869 was the last straw for some members, so about 30 families left to form an Orthodox congregation. Nevertheless, WHC grew and, in 1897, a larger building was erected on the same site.

By the 1930s and 1940s, as Jewish families left downtown Washington for suburban neighborhoods, the current site off Massachusetts Avenue was chosen for a new building. President Harry Truman laid the cornerstone in 1952 and President Dwight Eisenhower dedicated the temple in 1955. The congregation today has over 2,400 members. In addition to the synagogue on Macomb Street, the WHC runs a religious school in Potomac, Maryland.

In October 2019, the temple was vandalized with graffiti, including anti-Semitic statements, profane language, and drawings. It was not the first time the Washington Hebrew Congregation experienced a hate crime. A year earlier, after the deadly mass shooting at the Pittsburgh Tree of Life synagogue, a caller told the WHC temple receptionist, "I'm so glad that 11 people died at the other temple. I wanted you to know." According to the *Washington Post*, the phone call was one of 17 suspected anti-Semitic hate crimes in Washington, DC in 2018.

43. NBC Studio

One of the most famous TV personalities, known to children around the world, came to life in Tenleytown. In the mid-1950s, at the NBC-affiliated WRC-TV studio at 4001 Nebraska Avenue, University of Maryland student Jim Henson debuted Kermit the Frog on his show *Sam and Friends*. Henson made the puppet out of his mother's old green felt coat, using sliced ping pong balls for the bulbous eyes. Later versions improved upon the prototype, which one reporter described as more reptilian than amphibian.

the NBC studio at 4001 Nebraska Avenue sits on the site of the 18th-century estate Grassland

Jim and Jane Henson with Sam and Friends *characters Sam, Yorick, Kermit, and Harry the Hipster, circa 1956/57 (DC Public Library, Star Collection @ Washington Post)*

The studio was where John F. Kennedy and Richard Nixon held their second presidential debate on October 7, 1960. This time, Nixon looked better than in the first debate in Chicago when the majority of the 70 million television viewers perceived him as pale and sweaty. But he was still panned for using pancake makeup to cover a five o'clock shadow. Some pundits judged that the visual impression Nixon left in these debates cost him the election in what was a tight race.

Kennedy-Nixon debate at NBC studio, October 7, 1960 (Wikipedia Commons)

The Huntley-Brinkley Report partly originated at this studio in 1956, with Chet Huntley broadcasting and anchoring in New York and David Brinkley co-anchoring in Washington. Their daily send-off — "Good night, Chet. Good night, David. And good night, for NBC News." — became one of television's most famous catchphrases. The show ran until 1970, when Huntley retired. He was replaced by John Chancellor, and the show was recast as *NBC Nightly News.*

While most NBC shows are broadcast from the Rockefeller Center in New York, *Meet the Press* still takes place at the Nebraska Avenue studio. It has been running since 1947. *Meet the Press* was the first live television network news program to feature a sitting president: Gerald Ford in 1975.

David Brinkley (on screen from DC) and Chet Huntley in New York present The Huntley-Brinkley Report, *June 1963 (public domain)*

former Broadcast House, Brandywine & 40th Streets

The studio, now called NBC4, was built in Tenleytown to take advantage of its elevation. CBS affiliate WTOP also began broadcasting from Tenleytown in the mid-1950s, from Broadcast House on the corner of Brandywine Street and 40th Street NW.

The NBC studio is located at the site of the summer manor home, named Grassland, of Nathan Loughborough, who was Comptroller of the Treasury under President John Adams. Loughborough reportedly was the first resident of the District of Columbia to refuse to pay property taxes under the principle of no taxation without representation. (The slogan has not lost its poignancy.) A later owner, William Whitney, Secretary of the Navy under Grover Cleveland, caused a scandal when, while in office in 1887, he sold the 100-acre property for three times its purchase price.

44. Home of the Gecko

Until I saw the name spelled out, I did not know that the GEICO insurance company had a government connection. The corporate office of the Government Employees Insurance Company is in Chevy Chase, Maryland, just across the DC boundary, in the Friendship Village neighborhood.

Actually, GEICO is a private corporation, a wholly-owned subsidiary of Berkshire Hathaway, which is led by Warren Buffett, who, as mentioned in story 30, lived in Spring Valley as a teenager. GEICO does not have a formal government connection, but it started off selling auto insurance to federal government employees. It was founded in 1936 by Leo Goodwin, who had been working for USAA, which specializes in selling insurance to military personnel. Goodwin employed the same model in selling to feds, who as a group were deemed financially stable and risk averse. The headquarters in Chevy Chase was built in 1959.

In the mid-70s, when computerized driving records became available, the company began selling auto insurance to the general public, giving low rates to drivers with no recent accidents. Today GEICO is the second-largest auto insurer in the United States after State Farm.

Although number two in sales, GEICO is top in advertising, in terms of both spending and creativity. Everyone is familiar with the GEICO gecko, an advertising idea spawned by the way the company name was often mispronounced. For many years, this company mascot had a Cockney accent just to be different. GEICO has no connection to England, either.

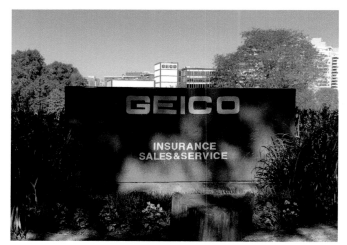

45.   Continuity of Government

Story 9 mentioned the distinctive brick water tower at Fort Reno, the highest elevation in the District of Columbia. In the picture below right, you can see three such towers. Only two of them are water towers: the one in the middle, built in 1903, and the one on the right with the French Norman design, built in 1928. The third, on the left, was the Cold War "Continuity of Government Tower" built in the early 1960s in a manner to blend in among the two preexisting water towers. Painted plexiglass at the top of the brick tower conceals a radar dish for top-secret communications linking Washington via microwave relay with the mid-Atlantic "federal relocation arc."

In the event of a Soviet nuclear attack, the facility, codenamed "Cartwheel" and manned around the clock, was supposed to function as the central spoke connecting whatever remained of the continuity of government system. Elevation was key because the microwave relay employed line of sight technology; the radar dishes at each relay literally had to be able to "see" one another. A network of similar towers was spaced out roughly fifty miles apart, allowing the signals to travel from Washington all the way to facilities in Pennsylvania.

construction of the radar tower in November 1961 (Dan Lewis, White House / John F. Kennedy Presidential Library and Museum)

Ft. Reno reservoir, radar tower (far left), and water towers

As characterized in an article about the tower in the Architect of the Capital website, "the whole thing was kind of ridiculous. Early civil defense concepts were based on outdated World War II era notions of air power, where an attack might constitute a single (relatively low yield) atomic bomb. By 1960, both the Soviet Union and the United States had developed intercontinental missiles that could carry vastly more powerful thermonuclear weapons. In the event of war several of these weapons may have been fired at Washington."

The communications system remains but is now used for civilian purposes by the Federal Aviation Administration, which took it over in the 1970s. When a reporter for a community newspaper asked the FAA about the tower in 1995, the answer was that it is an unmanned remote-transmitter site, to boost FAA handheld units (walkie-talkies). In case of emergency, the site can be activated to "direct aircraft."

46.   National Presbyterian Church

Two churches in our neighborhood include the title "national": the National Presbyterian Church at 4101 Nebraska Avenue and the National United Methodist Church down the street at 3401 Nebraska Avenue *(story 19)*. It does not mean that they are the national headquarters for their respective denominations. Rather, "national" means they represent their respective faiths in the nation's capital.

The National Presbyterian Church traces its history, through four congregations, to 1795, when Scottish stonemasons building the White House formed a church for worship services. Most Scottish immigrants to the New World were Presbyterian, thanks to John Knox taking John Calvin's reformation teachings back to Scotland in the 16th century.

In 1812, members from the White House stonemasons' group established the First Presbyterian Church on the south slope of Capitol Hill. A decade later, a new church was erected on 4½ Street NW. In the middle of the century, the senior pastor preached in favor of the abolition of slavery and allowed Frederick Douglass to speak from the church's pulpit. These were courageous acts in a city that was essentially a conservative Southern town at the time. In the mid-1920s, the city of Washington took the church's property under eminent domain for a new court system complex. In 1946, the congregation became the National Presbyterian Church. According to the church's website, most US presidents have attended services at the church or its predecessor buildings. The cornerstone of the present building was laid in 1967 by former President Eisenhower, who had been baptized in the church's predecessor building while he was serving in the White House. Although Donald Trump has been affiliated with Presbyterian churches, he is not known to have worshipped at the National Presbyterian Church.

Along with its soaring carillon tower, the church features a main sanctuary that seats 1,260 people. It is the third-largest religious center in Washington, after the National Cathedral and the Basilica of the National Shrine of the Immaculate Conception. An orphanage called the Hillcrest Children's Center once was located here. The National Presbyterian School and Child Care Center uses the renovated stone cottage left over from Hillcrest.

National Presbyterian School

In my first draft of a Facebook posting about the National Presbyterian Church and National Methodist Church, I found it difficult to explain the differences between the two faiths, with the former holding to predestination and the doctrine of grace, while Methodists believe salvation is given to those who have faith. My high school friend Tom Bracken offered the following yarn as an insight:

> A Presbyterian/Calvinist preacher and a Methodist pastor agree to swap pulpits one weekend. They meet each other in the woods riding horse to the other parson's church.
>
> The Presbyterian says: "Just imagine, God almighty planned from the beginning of time that I preach today to your parish about the glory of predestination."
>
> The Methodist preacher replied; "In that case, the deal's off — I ain't goin."

47.   Shroom House

The most striking house around is just across the DC-Maryland border, at 4949 Allan Rd.

The Shroom, as named on a sign by the door, looks like a setting for the *Flintstones* or *Lord of the Rings*. When originally built in 1923, the house was ordinary. In the 1970s, futurist architect Roy Mason redesigned it, using polyurethane foam to create the curvy shapes. Mason, who was based in Washington, DC, used similar techniques in other structures he designed, including a "Xanadu" house in Kissimmee, Florida, which became a popular tourist attraction. He was a founding member of the World Future Society and the publisher of *Futurist Magazine*. Mason created several forward-looking exhibits at the Capital Children's Museum, where he volunteered.

(Jill Schwartz Group)

The house has 6 bedrooms, 4 baths, and was last sold in 2018 for $1.5 million (not too much for homes near Tenleytown). The inside, renovated in 2015, is also whimsical.

48.   Fannie Mae

Given the comparisons often made between America's 2020 economic duress and the Great Depression, it may be interesting to look at one of the institutions founded under the New Deal.

With 20–25% of mortgages then in default, the federal government in 1938 established the Federal National Mortgage Association to provide local banks with federal money for financing home loans. Nicknamed Fannie Mae (a way of vocalizing its acronym FNMA), it succeeded in raising levels of home ownership by making mortgages more affordable. The key was creating a liquid secondary mortgage market. Helpful as this was to would-be homeowners, the practice was racially discriminatory. As recently as 1990, less than 3% of Fannie Mae's loans went to African American borrowers.

(Library of Congress)

In 1975, Fannie Mae purchased the Colonial Revival style headquarters of the Equitable Life Insurance Company at 3900 Wisconsin Avenue. Modeled after the Governor's Palace in Williamsburg, it was constructed in two phases in 1956–58 and 1963. The Historic Preservation Review Board in 2017 named it a historic landmark.

So, when Fannie Mae moved in 2018 to a downtown site that used to house the *Washington Post*, the redevelopers kept the existing structure. A 165-foot-tall oak tree in the front yard was moved and the basement is being enlarged to house DC's first Wegmans grocery store. The redevelopment plan, called the "Deal of the Year" in 2016 by the *Washington Business Journal*, will add eight new buildings, including a hotel and movie theater.

WAMU 88.5 American University Radio filmed the tree move in January 2019; Sidwell Friends is in the background (Jacob Fenston /WAMU)

49. Peter Muhlenberg

On Connecticut Avenue, a block south of Comet Pizza *(story 51)* stands a memorial to Peter Muhlenberg. Many of the 400 or so sculptures occupying public places in Washington were erected by local interest groups to honor favorite sons (and, very occasionally, daughters). This bust is one of them. Although the memorial and eponymous park in which it sits is owned and maintained by the National Park Service, it was donated by members of the adjacent St. Paul's Lutheran Church to honor this Lutheran minister, Revolutionary War hero, and early American politician. The project was started in 1928 but not finished until 1980.

Muhlenberg's life reads like a novel. Born to Pennsylvania German parents in 1746, he was sent at age 17 to Halle in the Germanic state of Saxony to be educated in Latin. Running away from the school, he served in a British infantry regiment and briefly in the German dragoons. This military experience was enough to win him appointment as a colonel in the Continental Army eight years later. But first he returned to Philadelphia for a classical education that prepared him to be ordained as a Lutheran minister. He then was asked to serve a congregation in the Shenandoah Valley, although he had to be ordained again, this time into the Anglican Church, which was the state church of the Virginia colony.

At the end of 1775, George Washington asked Muhlenberg to raise and command the 8th Virginia Regiment of the Continental Army. According to a biography written by his great-nephew, on January 21, 1776, Reverend Muhlenberg took his sermon text from Ecclesiastes 3, which starts with "To every thing there is a season." After reading the eighth verse, "a time of war, and a time of peace," he declared, "and this is the time of war," removing his clerical robe to reveal a colonel's uniform. Drums began to roll as 162 men reportedly walked down the aisle to enlist. Historians judge, however, that this story was greatly embellished, if not wholly invented, by Muhlenberg's fawning descendant.

As a brigadier general, Muhlenberg commanded a brigade at Valley Forge and fought in the Battle of Yorktown under the Marquis de Lafayette. At the end of the war, he settled in Montgomery County, Pennsylvania and soon was elected to a position under Benjamin Franklin comparable to that of Lieutenant Governor. Muhlenberg went on to be elected to the US House of Representatives, then to the US Senate, before being appointed by President Thomas Jefferson as the Supervisor of Revenue for Pennsylvania.

50.   Senator Feinstein's House

In 2001, California Senator Dianne Feinstein and her husband, San Francisco businessman Richard Blum bought the property at 3300 Nebraska Avenue, known as Willow Oaks. A glib magazine article said the "award-winning 1936 French Renaissance revival estate cost them a mere $5.6 million," $350,000 less than the asking price. It only has four bedrooms, but came with gorgeous gardens, a fully operational greenhouse, swimming pool, pool house, guesthouse, and carriage house.

Willow Oaks, 3300 Nebraska Ave.

*Senator Dianne Feinstein
(official portrait)*

Feinstein's house was the site of the private meeting on June 6, 2008 between Barack Obama and Hillary Clinton after he sewed up the Democratic Party presidential nomination at the end of a polarizing battle. According to CNN, "Feinstein left them in her living room with nothing other than water and comfortable chairs for what she called a positive meeting. No one else was in the room and no one is giving details of what was discussed." One reporter asked Feinstein if she heard any shouting. "No, they got along very well," she said.

Feinstein told the *New York Times*: "they want this opportunity privately, you know. You all know what it's like, I mean, you go out, you have to make a statement, and there are press, and everybody is critical of it. And they just want an opportunity to meet together alone." She added: "And you know, this is a deeply personal time too. You are sorting out your feelings. Hillary is going to be giving a big speech tomorrow. Barack is trying to put things together for a major presidential campaign. So, there are a lot of decompression, nerve endings, all these things that need to kind of come together and I think the opportunity to sit down, just the two of them, have an hour together was positive."

The next day, Clinton formally conceded and endorsed Obama.

51.   #Pizzagate

This is an exceedingly strange story, which keeps getting weirder.

A funky pizzeria at 5037 Connecticut Avenue used to be known most of all for its calzone, its ping pong tables, and its live music that sometimes went beyond midnight to the annoyance of a few neighbors. But in early December 2016, Comet Pizza, as it is commonly called, became known nationally for something else.

On a pleasant Sunday afternoon, a man walked into the restaurant armed with a revolver, knife, and semi-automatic rifle. As he searched the premises, he fired three rifle rounds (not hitting anyone, fortunately). The shooter, Edgar Welch, told police that he drove up from North Carolina to "self-investigate" outrageous claims circulating in fringe social media platforms that Hillary Clinton and other Democratic Party figures were running a child sex-trafficking ring in tunnels under the restaurant. Welch surrendered to police after realizing no children were being held at the pizzeria and that it does not even have a basement.

How on earth did the debunked "Pizzagate" theme emerge and grow to the point of sparking a near mass murder in our innocent community? The hysteria started with a tweet linking Clinton to pedophilia in late October 2016, two days after then-FBI Director James Comey told Congress that he was reopening the investigation of her use of a private email server. The mad notion spread to 4chan and Reddit through anonymous posts, then was picked up by talk-show host Alex Jones on the far-right site Infowars. In a YouTube video posted on November 4th that was viewed almost half a million times, Jones talked about "all the children Hillary Clinton has personally murdered and chopped up and raped."

The hashtag #Pizzagate first appeared on Twitter three days after that video posting and was retweeted hundreds of thousands of times each day, disproportionately from the Czech Republic, Cyprus, and Vietnam, most frequently by bots — telltale signs of a Russian connection. With #Pizzagate trending, the preposterous rumor spread like wildfire, to be picked up by armed deviants.

This was all crazy, of course. The owner of the pizzeria had held a fundraiser at Comet Pizza for the Clinton campaign, and John Podesta, chair of the campaign, had been known to dine at Comet. Oh, and Clinton had once eaten at the French bistro Terasol across the street and had her picture taken with the owner and the owner's daughter. Based on that posted photo, the conspiracy nuts concluded that Terasol was also involved in a plot to abuse children. Up the block, the Politics and Prose bookstore was added to the mix, with claims that it was linked by underground tunnels to

Comet Pizza. The fact that one of the bookstore's co-owners had worked for many years as Hillary Clinton's speechwriter and adviser became another data point in the so-called Pizzagate. The bookstore had to fend off over a hundred threatening phone calls a day.

When Welch was sentenced in June 2017 to four years in prison for assault and a federal firearms charge, you'd think it would have been the end of Pizzagate. Yet conspiracy fanatics just changed their claims, to now say he was a government plant engaged in a false-flag plot to conceal the truth.

Then, in January 2019, an arsonist set a fire in Comet Pizza, which was quickly put out by employees. Two weeks later, Ryan Jaselskis, who fit the CCTV image of the perpetrator to a T, was arrested for climbing over a fence surrounding the Washington Monument and fighting with officers. Initially, there was no indication that he was linked to the 2016 shooting incident. But on the day the fire was set, a YouTube page in the name of his parents posted a video promoting the crazy QAnon theory about a "storm" that supposedly will come when President Donald Trump makes public the arrests of those behind a child sex-trafficking cabal and the "deep state." In December 2019, Jaselskis pleaded guilty to the arson and assault on a federal law enforcement officer. Police and court documents do not state a motive.

Those who egged on these terrorists have gone unpunished and unrepentant. Before Twitter banned the hashtag in mid-2020, searching "Pizzagate" brought up dozens of hits, including unspecified accusations against Barack Obama, picking up on Trump's "Obamagate" Twitter storm from May 10, 2020. An article in the *Washingtonian* magazine on May 11, 2020 said, "Comet Ping Pong has been getting a new uptick in Pizzagate messages." The lesson of the story is that, however absurd, false accusations circulated on the internet have real-world consequences.

Map — Cleveland Park

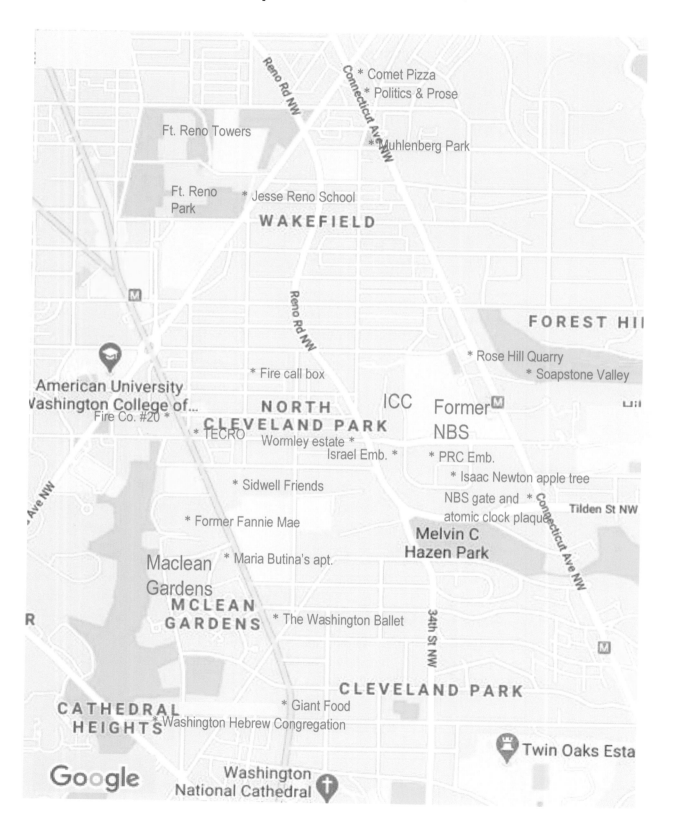

Part IV: Diplomacy and Espionage

52.   International Chancery Center

For many years, foreign countries preferred to establish their representative offices relatively close to the White House, near Dupont Circle and Logan Circle, repurposing private mansions. Location was important in order to fulfill the diplomat's central role of cultivating contacts and gathering information. The renowned journalist Edward R. Murrow said the key to international exchange is "the last three feet," meaning the person-to-person contact. The coronavirus shutdown of 2020 made the job far more difficult.

As the city expanded after the Civil War and outlying areas became more fashionable and accessible, many embassies moved to more distant locations. In the 1900s, sections of 16th Street and, later, Massachusetts Avenue both took the nickname as Embassy Row. The higher ground of Kalorama also became a hub for embassies, drawn to its cooler air. (Today, the Obamas live in Kalorama as do Jared Kushner and Ivanka Trump .)

Before World War II, Washington, DC was home to 56 embassies. This number expanded after the war, as the United States took on world power responsibilities and more nations became independent. Some of the new states found it hard to secure property; residents in Chevy Chase and other desirable residential neighborhoods wanted nothing to do with the premium curbside parking that embassies required and the noisy functions they hosted. However, when the Vienna Convention on Diplomatic and Consular Relations came into effect in 1964, the US government became obliged to provide suitable and affordable space for foreign missions.

To meet the terms of the Vienna Convention, Congress passed a law which allocated a tract of low-cost federal land for a purpose-built embassy enclave called the International Chancery Center (ICC). A chancery is the main building of an embassy, which might also have separate buildings for consular, cultural, and other functions. The ICC, located on both sides of Van Ness Street between Reno Road and Connecticut Avenue, is also home to the State Department's Office of Foreign Missions. There are also three parks on this 47-acre, federally owned hilltop property, which was previously occupied by the National Bureau of Standards *(story 14)*.

The chanceries at the ICC must be designed to reflect the national heritage and style of their respective homelands. In addition to the Office of Foreign Missions, both the National Capital Planning Commission and the Commission of Fine Arts must review and approve the architectural plans submitted by each foreign government.

The ICC was established in 1972, but it took time to persuade foreign governments to occupy a seemingly isolated enclave. The State of Israel in 1979 became the first to take a lease there *(story 53)*. Over the next several decades, 16 other countries filled up the allotted one-acre plots. The character of the complex became strongly Islamic, as ten of the 17 parcels were leased by the predominantly Muslim states of Bahrain, Bangladesh, Brunei, Egypt, Jordan, Kuwait, Malaysia, Morocco, Pakistan, and the United Arab Emirates.

Until about 1900, foreign missions to and from the United States were called legations, which have a lower rank than embassies and are headed by ministers rather than ambassadors. Until the end of the 19th century, an "ambassador" was considered to be the monarch's personal representative, meaning that only kingdoms sent and received them. After Emperor Napoleon III was toppled in 1870, the new French Third Republic continued the French Empire's practice of designating and hosting ambassadors. The United States then followed this practice in 1893.

A total of 193 nations maintain formal diplomatic relations with the United States. Of these, 176 have embassies in the capital. (Nine other tiny states are represented in New York City.) Washington, DC also hosts delegations from the African Union and the European Union, while Taiwan is present via an economic and cultural representative office *(story 55)*. The former embassy of Iran, at 3005 Massachusetts Avenue, is maintained by the Department of State, while Pakistan, as Iran's "protecting power" in America, hosts the Iranian Interests section in its embassy.

A new enclave of 11–15 foreign embassies is planned for a 32-acre portion of the former Walter Reed Army Medical Center on 16th Street and Alaska Avenue, which will be called the Foreign Missions Center.

Here are photos of most of the embassies at the International Chancery Center.

Embassy of United Arab Emirates

Embassy of Morocco

Embassy of Egypt

Embassy of Jordan

Embassy of Brunei

Embassy of Austria

Embassy of Bahrain

Embassy of Kuwait

Embassy of Pakistan

Embassy of Bangladesh

Embassy of Slovakia

Embassy of Singapore

Embassy of Ethiopia

Embassy of Malaysia

Embassy of Ghana

53.   Israeli Embassy

As the first country to take advantage of the land that the US government made available for embassies at International Chancery Center *(story 52)*, Israel was given the corner lot at Van Ness Street and Reno Road, with the address of 3514 International Drive. Groundbreaking was timed for Israeli Independence Day, May 1979, and the new embassy was unveiled the next year.

The beautiful buff-colored brick building reflects Jerusalem's contemporary architecture, with arches crowning deeply recessed windows and all floors facing inward onto an atrium that conveys natural light into the building. The ironwork features a menorah (candelabrum), the traditional national symbol.

The architects had to resist pressure from security officers for more massiveness and enclosure. There is no shortage of security measures, however. The chancery is protected by cameras, motion and sound sensors, a steel fence, a locked gate, a guardhouse, a brick wall, and a heavy steel cable to thwart truck bombers.

The embassy is often the site of protests concerning Palestine. There was also an internal protest one day in October 2019, when the building, along with Israeli embassies all over the world, was closed as a complaint by employees over a Finance Ministry decision to tax financial allowances for working overseas. The one-day work stoppage was a positive example of Israeli democracy in action.

side view of Israeli Embassy, from Van Ness Street

The Israeli Embassy was also once the scene of a thrilling spy chase. On November 21, 1985, US Navy intelligence analyst Jonathan Pollard and his wife, Anne, tried to drive through the embassy's security gate by tailgating an Israeli diplomat's car. The Pollards had realized they were being surveilled by the FBI and the Naval Intelligence Service (NIS, which in 1992 changed its name to Naval Criminal Investigative Service) and wanted to claim asylum. Israeli security guards blocked the car, however, and moments later the feds showed up to arrest the pair. The NIS had become suspicious because Pollard was handling large amounts of classified information that had nothing to do with the regions for which he had analytical responsibility.

Jonathan Pollard
(US Navy I.D. picture)

Pollard had been spying for Israel for the previous 16 months, providing some 800 publications and more than 1,000 US government cables. Several times a week, he loaded his briefcase with documents for delivery to the Israelis, who copied and returned them. They paid Pollard, who had the codename Hunting Horse, a monthly $2,500 stipend, cash for expensive vacations, an engagement ring for Anne, and other rewards.

In 1987, Pollard was convicted and became the only person ever to receive a life sentence for spying on the United States on behalf of a country considered to be an ally. Although Israeli authorities initially denied any involvement, they acknowledged in 1998 that he had been an Israeli asset and granted him citizenship. They also unsuccessfully lobbied the US government at the highest levels for many years to seek his freedom. He was a point of diplomatic tension, as well as a dubious *cause célèbre* for many ardent supporters of Israel.

Pollard contended that he only supplied Israel with information critical to its security and that what had influenced him to do so was the alleged anti-Israeli attitudes of his intelligence community colleagues. The US intelligence community firmly opposed any clemency for Pollard, maintaining that the damage he caused to US national security was far more severe than publicly acknowledged and that his motivation was not concern for Israeli security but personal greed.

In betraying the United States, Pollard offered his services to four other countries besides Israel. Even if he had only spied for Israel, however, most experts say Pollard would still have deserved strict punishment for selling crucial US secrets. He eventually was released on parole in 2015 in accordance with federal guidelines in place at the time of his sentencing. Following his conviction, Israel insisted it stopped espionage activities in the United States. There would be no more "friends spying on friends," although as we will see in story 67, at least one other would-be spy has sought to follow Pollard's path.

54. PRC Embassy

The largest of the chanceries at International Chancery Center, occupying three of its lots and situated more or less at the center of the others, is the embassy of the People's Republic of China (PRC). Built in 2008, it was designed by an architecture firm founded by sons of I. M. Pei, who served as a consultant. The 300,000-square-foot building is meant to be a symbol of China's economic power. It took years of negotiation with the State Department to arrange the lease in a deal that allowed a reciprocal site for a new US embassy in Beijing. The PRC has the largest number of accredited diplomats in Washington, taking up seven and a half pages of the 136-page diplomatic list. (Canada and Saudi Arabia, next largest, each take up five and a half pages.)

The PRC embassy's address is 3505 International Place. Senator Ted Cruz has been trying for several years to rename the street after Chinese dissident Liu Xiaobo. This would make the embassy's new address "1 Liu Xiaobo Plaza." Liu, who died in 2017, was a Nobel Peace Prize laureate who called for an end to communist one-party rule and was repeatedly imprisoned for his efforts. He is a worthy man to honor, although if Cruz's bill ever became law, you can bet that China would retaliate by naming the street in front of the US embassy in Beijing something offensive. Suggestions floated on Chinese social media have included "Edward Snowden Street" and "Osama bin Laden Road." In the photo below, the tent houses protestors from the persecuted Falun Gong spiritual movement. When I went up to talk to them, they claimed China is still murdering members of the group and harvesting their organs for sale for transplant, as reported by Reuters in 2019.

To end on a positive note, Ambassador Cui Tiankai represents his country well. When I called on him at the impressive embassy in 2017 along with the head of my institute, Cui listened and made appropriate promises, even if they did not pan out. In March 2020, Cui disavowed a conspiracy theory promoted by Foreign Ministry spokesman Zhao Lijian that the coronavirus was created and spread by the US military.

People's Republic of China Embassy

back of PRC Embassy, from Van Ness St.

55. Representing Taiwan

I have long been fond of Taiwan, visiting it five times to date. Kyoko and I went there from Japan on our honeymoon in 1976. We went back in 1980 from our diplomatic posting in Seoul. In 2015, I was invited to lead a small group of British-based academics on a friendship-building tour.

Taipei Economic and Cultural Representative Office, 4201 Wisconsin Ave.

It is hard not to feel friendly toward this democratic, vibrant, and well-functioning island, especially when it is bullied by mainland China. For example, despite having one of the first exposures to COVID-19 and one of the best responses to the virus, Taiwan has been prevented from attending meetings of the World Health Organization, due to pressure from Beijing.

The residents of Taiwan increasingly see themselves as a separate people. Mainland authorities, on the other hand, consider Taiwan to be a runaway province and regard reunification as essential to fully realizing China's rightful position in the world. PRC representatives protest when they hear anybody call Taiwan a country, suggest it should be independent, or hint at improving political ties with it.

We all remember when Nixon went to China in 1972. He signed the Shanghai Communique, in which the PRC stated its "one-China principle" that Taiwan is part of China and would eventually be reunified. Washington used the communique to state its own one-China policy, which acknowledged Beijing's position that there is but one China and that Taiwan is part of it. It is a diplomatic way of saying, "Yes, we hear you." It implicitly accepted Taiwan's future merger with China as long as it was accomplished peacefully.

A few years later, in 1979, Washington switched recognition from the Republic of China, based in Taiwan, to the PRC. This was during the Sino-Soviet split. Recognizing the PRC was a way to counter Soviet political influence and perceived military threat. Most other countries did the same. Beijing has not been coy about using its economic might to continue to pressure small countries to follow suit.

Today, the 24 million people living in the free part of "one China" are represented in Washington by the Taipei Economic and Cultural Representative Office (TECRO) at 4201 Wisconsin Avenue. Not flying a flag outside and only displaying a small sign, Taiwan's diplomatic headquarters in the United States can be mistaken for a run-of-the-mill office building. From its internet link, taiwanembassy.org, you can see what the Taiwan government considers it to be.

The Taiwan government also owns the Twin Oaks estate in Cleveland Park, whose 18-acre grounds are larger than the White House compound. The estate's 26-room English Georgian Renaissance-style mansion was built in 1888 and was once the home of Gardiner Greene Hubbard, first president of the National Geographic Society and father-in-law of Alexander Graham Bell, the inventor of the telephone. After renting the property for ten years as the official residence of its ambassadors, the Republic of China purchased the estate from the Hubbard family in 1947. Madame Chiang Kai-shek stayed here during her visits to Washington, DC in the 1950s and 60s. TECRO still uses it for entertaining.

Twin Oaks (Daniel Liao, TECRO)

front gate of Twin Oaks, 3225 Woodley Rd.

56. Brazilian Army Commission

Washington, DC is full of diplomatic properties. In addition to the 176 foreign embassies, there are representative offices, ambassador residences, consular sections, trade offices, and various annexes. Being considered foreign soil, they are exempt from zoning and building codes and property taxes when directly owned by the foreign government. But while our city is therefore missing out on a lot of tax revenue, a study for the National Capital Planning Commission found that "foreign missions represent a critical component of the international business industry."

Two buildings at 4632 and 4706 Wisconsin Avenue exemplify the ancillary forms that diplomatic missions can take. They are the Brazilian Army Commission and its Annex, sitting unnoticed to many passers-by in between real estate offices and small restaurants. The two offices, housing 45 staff, are owned by the Brazilian government.

Brazilian Army Commission and its Annex, 4632 and 4706 Wisconsin Ave.

As World War II escalated, the Brazilian Military Mission in DC was established in April 1940 to procure high-caliber cannons and other war material. Meant to be temporary, the mission became permanent after the war, as Brazil's defense and foreign policies became closely aligned with the United States. The commission moved to Wisconsin Avenue in about 1990. In addition to procuring equipment for the Brazilian defense forces, the commission conducts market research and supports the military attaché's office at the embassy itself, two and a half miles away on Massachusetts Avenue.

57. Russian Embassy

The Russian Embassy at 2650 Wisconsin Avenue has seen its share of controversy. When the Soviet Union took over the property in 1985, the US government was heavily criticized for allowing its nemesis to occupy one of the highest vantage points in the city. Mount Alto, as the site is called, has an elevation of 351 feet and provides a sweeping view of downtown DC, including the White House and State Department. More important than the panoramic views, the location is ideal for electronic surveillance of microwave communications. "We just got snookered; it's inexplicable," New York Senator Daniel Patrick Moynihan complained.

The move to the 10-acre property, which previously housed a Veterans Administration hospital *(story 32)*, was in accordance with a US-Soviet deal cut in 1969, when the technology to intercept microwave transmissions was little understood. In exchange for giving the Soviets an 85-year lease on the Mount Alto site, the United States was allowed to move its embassy in Moscow closer to the Kremlin.

2619 Wisconsin Ave, where some think, probably incorrectly, that the tunnel started

In 1985, US officials discovered that the KGB had embedded dozens of listening devices in the foundation of the new American Embassy in Moscow. The effort to remove them cost $250 million. Meanwhile, beginning in the late 1970s, the FBI and the National Security Agency were carrying out their own eavesdropping plan by digging a secret tunnel for electronic surveillance under the Soviet chancery. While some think the tunnel began at a house across Wisconsin Avenue, most likely it was from a now-demolished house on Fulton Street north of the embassy compound. Operation Monopoly, which took ten years and cost hundreds of millions of dollars, never produced any information of value because FBI traitor Robert Hanssen told the KGB about the operation. For his betrayal, Hanssen was sentenced to 15 consecutive life sentences.

The Mount Alto compound, which cost $70 million to build, includes an eight-story white marble chancery, a four-story consulate and ambassador's residence, a reception hall, a 165-unit apartment building, a school for Russian diplomats' children, a gymnasium, and a 400-seat auditorium. Due to my previous position heading the Washington office of a London-based think tank, I and my wife have been invited to several cultural events there. Such occasions often attract small demonstrations on the sidewalk protesting human rights violations in Russia.

In 2018, the Council of the District of Columbia designated the section of Wisconsin Avenue in front of the embassy as "Boris Nemtsov Plaza," in honor of a democracy activist who was killed on a bridge near the Kremlin in 2015. When critics of the Russian regime failed to pass a law in Congress so naming the street, the effort was brought to the DC council instead. The measure is largely symbolic, as the street address for the embassy remained unchanged.

A similar symbolic protest took place in 1984, when Congress voted to change the name of a block of 16th Street NW outside the then-Soviet Embassy to "Andrei Sakharov Plaza," in homage to the Soviet Union's best-known dissident. The building became the ambassador's residence when the embassy moved to Mount Alto.

The Beaux-Arts mansion on 16th Street has a fabled history. It was built in 1910 by Hattie Pullman, widow of the founder of the sleeping-car company, as a home for her daughter and son-in-law, a congressman. Because he fell ill before moving in, however, the building was sold in 1913 to Russia's Czar Nicholas II. After the 1917 Bolshevik Revolution, the ambassador fled to Paris with the best paintings and furniture from the building. The structure stood empty until 1933, when President Franklin Roosevelt granted diplomatic recognition to the Soviet Union. As the *Washingtonian* put it, the chancery "became known for vodka and caviar, secretive ways, and a rooftop collection of antennas." Little has changed.

1125 16th St. NW, Russian ambassador's residence

58. Caribbean Integration

On a list of embassies in Washington in early 2020, I was pleased to see that four had addresses in a building close to American University called the Caribbean Chancery. They are familiar countries, most of which my wife and I visited before the coronavirus made cruise ships untenable. The embassies of Dominica, Saint Kitts and Nevis, Saint Lucia, and Saint Vincent and the Grenadines were all said to be located at 3216 New Mexico Avenue NW. The consortium of small Caribbean nations acquired the building from Finland when that country moved its embassy to a modern chancery on Massachusetts Avenue in 1994.

former Caribbean Chancery, 3216 New Mexico Ave.

When I walked by, however, the building was deserted and not because of the pandemic. A plaque on the right front gate was missing and a shabby one on the left said "OECS Building (Organization of East Caribbean States)." It turns out that the embassies moved in 2019 to an office building on K Street and that the OECS itself is not represented in Washington.

Established in 1981 by seven founding countries, the OECS today has added four associate members. All of the members are tiny in terms of both area and population. The overriding purpose of the organization is to promote regional integration to take advantage of economies of scale. The OECS members share a common market, a central bank, a currency (East Caribbean dollar), and a regional assembly of parliamentarians. There are greater economies of scale in the larger Caribbean Community (CARICOM), established in 1973 and which today comprises fifteen nations and dependencies and five associate members. Unlike the OECS however, CARICOM does not have a common currency or monetary union.

Neither grouping has carried integration as far as envisioned. According to the International Monetary Fund, further liberalizing trade and labor mobility in the Caribbean could generate significant economic benefits, but implementation of integration initiatives toward the goal of a regional economic union has been slow. The individual states do not want to surrender their sovereignty.

Lack of political will for integration has been the story for decades. In 1958, the United Kingdom oversaw the formation of the West Indies Federation as a political union of ten Caribbean territories that were British colonies, with the intention of it becoming a confederated state like the early Canadian Confederation. Five other Caribbean territories opted not to join, in the belief that their future lay with association with North America or Central America. Four years later the West Indies Federation fell apart when Jamaica, which was much larger than the other members and located further west, decided to leave. The next largest state, Trinidad and Tobago, then decided to leave as well. The premier of that country quipped "one from ten leaves nought" — in other words, without Jamaica, no federation was possible.

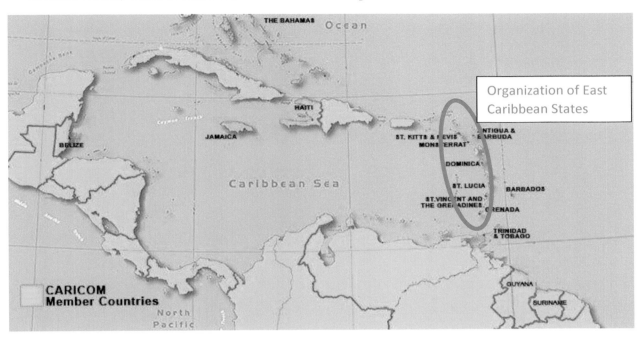

(KnowledgeWalk Institute, "Caribbean Community (CARICOM)," with OECS group added)

One thing CARICOM does have going for it is an anthem, selected in a 2014 competition. The winning entry, by Michele Henderson of Dominica, celebrates the history, culture and identity of the people of the Caribbean. I am not sure, however, how much it has contributed to the push for greater integration.

Dominica's Michele Henderson
(courtesy of the songstress; 365 Photography)

59. South Korean Ambassador's Residence

When the American Ambassador's residence in Seoul was re-built in 1974 in the style of a traditional Korean home, it inspired the Republic of Korea (ROK or South Korea) to build its own ambassador's residence in Washington in a Korean architectural style. The 1980s building, bordering the southwest corner of the AU campus at 4801 Glenbrook Drive, does this magnificently. I first visited it in 1988, when I was the North Korea Desk Officer at the State Department.

(Courtesy of Embassy of the Republic of Korea)

Although the word "embassy" commonly means the offices where the ambassador and staff work, the original meaning of where an ambassador lives is occasionally still used. An article about Spring Valley, for example, said there are "over two dozen foreign embassies" in the neighborhood, by which the author meant embassy residences.

Because I am a board member of the Korea Economic Institute of America and a frequent commentator about Korean security issues, I

(Above and right by Mayet Pascual, Oct. 7, 2019)

am still sometimes invited to the ROK ambassador's residence. It is pleasant on the receptions for National Foundation Day in early October when guests are welcomed into the well-sculptured garden, where bulgogi is grilled in a curved recess lit by stone lanterns.

(Mayet Pascual, Oct. 7, 2019)

The back garden was not always inviting, however. It is the site of a circa-1918 bomb burial pit when chemical weapons were developed at American University (the worst part of that pit was next door, as discussed in story 29). After it was discovered in 1998, the Army Corps of Engineers clean-up removed 623 pieces of bombs, shells, bottles of chemicals, metal drums, and other debris from the residence garden. Fourteen items still had chemical warfare agent, the Army said, and mustard gas and arsenic had leaked from some of the shells. Jim Kelman, a State Department official from the then Nonproliferation Bureau, recalls attending a reception at the residence at the beginning of the millennium. Upon presenting his business card in the receiving line, the ambassador welcomed Jim by saying: "food is in the courtyard, drinks along the patio, and WMD [weapons of mass destruction] in the back yard."

Trees, plants, and two feet of soil were removed and replaced before the property could be declared arsenic-free. The garden is now better than ever. The residence itself is magnificent. The large painting in the reception hall, shown behind Congressman Gerry Connolly in the below photo, was done by the Modernist Lee Dai-Won (1921–2005), who managed the Bando art gallery Seoul in the 1960s. One of his paintings sold for over half a million dollars.

Rep. Gerry Connolly at ROK ambassador's residence celebrating Korea's National Foundation Day, October 4, 2018 (Hyun Lee)

60.   Japanese Ambassador's Residence

Considering my two postings as a US diplomat in Japan, the beautiful building at 4000 Nebraska Avenue is right up my alley. It is also just down the street and around the corner from our house.

front entrance at 4000 Nebraska Ave.

A 2019 article in the magazine *Capital File* introduces the site: "Hidden inconspicuously on eight acres off Nebraska Avenue in American University Park is a Japanese-styled attraction that gets much less attention than the annual Cherry Blossom Festival — the elegant residence of the Japanese ambassador." The residence was designed by architect Isoya Yoshida and completed in 1977. Before that, the Japanese ambassador made do with a Neo-Georgian style house next to the embassy on Massachusetts Avenue.

Four Seasons by Kayama Matazo in the dining room (Embassy of Japan)

koi pond in front of teahouse (Embassy of Japan)

Ambassador Shinsuke Sugiyama, appointed in 2018, told *Capital Style*: "The house is an amazing architectural artwork…. The collection at the residence creates a sort of museum that introduces guests to some of the styles and techniques used by Japan's greatest artists, including some who were honored by my country as living national treasures." Befitting Japanese taste for simplicity, the architect mandated that each room have just one piece of art.

reception room (Embassy of Japan)

koi pond (Embassy of Japan)

Kyoko at garden party, July 6, 2019

Kyoko and I have been lucky enough to be invited to several receptions there, including to a garden party in summer 2019, when guests were strongly encouraged to wear casual summer clothes rather than diplomatic finery.

I posted this story on Facebook on May 2, 2020, the 44th anniversary of when another beautiful Japanese building was the backdrop to the most significant event in my life.

wedding at Shimogamo Shrine, Kyoto, May 2, 1976

61.   Swedish Ambassador's Residence

Next to the Japanese ambassador's residence is an even larger plot of land at 3900 Nebraska Avenue which has been used for the residence of the Swedish ambassador. The Spanish Colonial-style house was built in the 1940s by architect Arthur B. Heaton, who was the first supervising architect of the National Cathedral *(story 13)*. It was built for the founder of *U.S. News & World Report*, David F. Lawrence, who in 1950 sold it to the Swedish Embassy. Those were the days when publishing was a lucrative business.

(Carol M. Highsmith Archive, Library of Congress,
Prints and Photographs Division)

back garden (Ted Stuebner)

Countess Ulla Wachtmeister decorated the residence with rugs, furniture, art, and wallpaper by Swedish artists when her husband, Count Wilhelm Wachtmeister, was ambassador from 1974 to 1989. For the last four of those 15 years, he was the longest-serving ambassador in Washington, making him dean of the ambassador corps. Diplomats normally serve three to four years. Count Wachtmeister was given a much longer tenure, due to his connections and to his success in patching up strained relations after the Vietnam War years. In 1972, Prime Minister Olof Palme labeled President Nixon a war criminal akin to the Nazis for ordering the bombing of Cambodia, in response to which the United States froze relations for many months.

Since the mid-1970s, Sweden-US relations have been good, albeit with an occasional, shall we say, "rocky" patch. In June 2019, American rapper A$AP Rocky was arrested over a physical altercation in Stockholm. In several tweets, US President Trump demanded that he be released. The Swedish Prime Minister's office responded that it was not allowed to influence legal proceedings and that in Sweden "everyone is equal before the law."

The large garden is considered to be one of the best private gardens in the city, although it is mostly lawn. President George H.W. Bush often played tennis at the court at the bottom of the garden with Ambassador Wachtmeister. Few ambassadors had better connections.

I have not seen the house or the garden, except through the surrounding chain-link fence. Now, I will probably never get the opportunity, because the Swedish government has decided to sell the property and to move the residence to the House of Sweden, home of the Embassy of Sweden (and of Iceland), next to Georgetown's Washington Harbour.

The *Washington Post* called House of Sweden "a far cry from the city's other fenced, bunkerlike embassies." The only embassy ever built on the Potomac River, it has scenic

FIFA World Cup Viewing Party, Sweden vs. Germany, June 2018 (Embassy of Sweden)

views and is scenic itself, especially at night, when it is transformed into a translucent glass box. Drawing 30,000 guests a year, it is a popular venue for embassy-sponsored concerts, movie nights, art exhibits, and seminars designed to enhance Sweden's image. Each year, the embassy selects a theme reflecting "Swedish values," such as migration or gender equality, and shapes its events around that topic. The 2020 theme has been innovation and mobility.

public use area of Sweden House (Åke E:son Lindman)

House of Sweden (Embassy of Sweden)

62.   Yemeni Ambassador's Residence

One of the poorest countries in the world has a pricey ambassador's residence. Since 2015, Yemen has been wracked by civil war and foreign interventions that have displaced millions of its people. Yemen already had a dire shortage of potable water and now is caught by the pandemic. In 2019, the UN described Yemen as the world's worst humanitarian crisis. A United Nations Development Program report says that if fighting continues through 2022, Yemen will rank as the poorest country in the world, with 79% of the population living under the poverty line and 65% classified as extremely poor. Death, dust, and destruction is the common image.

By contrast, the ambassador of Yemen to the United States finds refuge in leafy, toney Spring Valley. By some estimates, his residence at 4850 Glenbrook Road has a current market value of over $10 million. It sits on a 1.3-acre wooded lot with a stream in front accented by a quaint bridge. Built in 1942 and renovated in 2009, it has six bedrooms and six and a half bathrooms.

Yemeni ambassador's residence, 4850 Glenbrook Rd.

Spanish Ambassador to OAS

If you go by, take a look as well across the street. Diagonally across from the Yemeni ambassador, the Permanent Resident Ambassador of Spain to the Organization of American States (OAS) lives at 4901 Glenbrook Road in a house with five bedrooms and four baths, with an estimated value of $4.1 million. When I saw flagpoles on the lawn flying the Spanish and European Union flags, I first assumed it was the ambassador's residence, but he lives at a much swankier place on Foxhall Road. So, I knocked on the door and learned that Spain has more than one ambassador in Washington, DC.

63.   Mexican Ambassador's Residence

An article in the *Washington Diplomat* in 2017 said the Mexican ambassador "may very well have the toughest job on Embassy Row." The next line in the article laid it on: "After all, what training prepares any ambassador to represent a country — an ally and neighbor of the United States, no less — whose people are continually insulted, ridiculed, and dumped on by none other than the chief occupant of the Oval Office?" Ambassador Gerónimo Gutiérrez Fernández (who left in 2018) diplomatically told the journal "It's been intense. It's been interesting." Having seen the tweets and heard the rally applause lines, you know what he means.

Mexican ambassador's residence, 4925 Loughboro Rd.

In addition to managing the fraught bilateral relationship, the Mexican ambassador oversees 21 consulates general and 30 consulates across the United States. (Consulates general, usually located in major cities, provide less of a full range of services than do consulates.) In Washington, in addition to the chancery at 1911 Pennsylvania Avenue NW, Mexico's diplomatic presence in Washington consists of the Mexican Cultural Institute on 16th Street, a consular office on 23rd Street, the ambassador's residence at 4925 Loughboro Road, and, at an adobe-style building at 2440 Massachusetts Avenue, the Permanent Mission of Mexico to the Organization of American States.

The residence is a stately 11,000-square-foot home on two acres set off from the busy road. Acquired by the Mexican government in 1973, it has seven bedrooms, six fireplaces, and five and a half baths. It is estimated to be worth up to $9.1 million.

The current ambassador, Martha Bárcena Coqui, appointed by President Andrés Manuel López Obrador in January 2019, is among the cream of the crop of the Mexican diplomatic corps. She earned academic degrees from schools in Rome, Madrid, and Mexico City and has been a professor of national security and diplomacy. Earlier in life, she was a professional ballet dancer. Married to a retired diplomat, Bárcena, in addition to Spanish, speaks English, French, and Italian.

In Washington, Bárcena's top priority has been on renegotiating the North American Free Trade Agreement. In July 2020, she oversaw a visit to Washington by President López Obrador to meet with President Donald Trump to mark the revised trade deal among the United States, Mexico, and Canada that took effect that month.

Ambassador Martha Bárcena Coqui (Sergio Ochoa, Embassy of Mexico in the USA)

President López Obrador exchanges baseball bats with President Donald Trump at the White House on July 8, 2020 (Sergio Ochoa, Embassy of Mexico in the USA)

Ugandan Ambassador's Residence

If you are doing a walking tour, you may want to extend it further down the road to 5009 Loughboro Road, residence of the ambassador of Uganda. The 5,600-square-foot house has six bedrooms and seven baths and is valued at $3.4 million. Uganda has had an embassy in the United States since becoming independent in 1962. It stayed open when the US closed its embassy in Uganda from 1973 to 1979 over threats to Americans when Idi Amin was president. Relations later stabilized, although the United States cut aid in 2014 in response to Uganda's outlawing of homosexuality. US aid has since resumed and in 2019 reached nearly $1 billion.

Uganda ambassador's residence, 5009 Loughboro Rd.

64. Code-busters

At 3801 Nebraska Avenue is the former Mount Vernon Seminary for Girls that today serves as headquarters of the Department of Homeland Security. During World War II, the US Navy took over the campus for secret "essential wartime activities." The campus fit the Navy's needs: located away from tall buildings; situated on high ground with clear sightlines to the Pentagon and other military installations; and having a group of buildings that could be immediately put to Navy use. It was named the Naval Communications Annex.

A critical part of the workforce was a contingent of 3,000 WAVES (Women Accepted for Voluntary Emergency Service) who operated crypto-analytic equipment that helped break German and Japanese communications codes. WAVES were sworn to secrecy and told that discussion of their work outside of approved channels could mean facing the death penalty for treason. When friends or family members asked about their job, they were taught to say "We just push a pencil like everybody else." Due in part to their efforts, the Allies broke the German Enigma code in 1944 and thereby soon were able to cripple the German submarine fleet. The WAVES also helped break the Japanese code.

 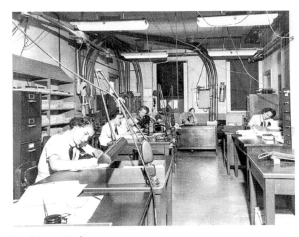

(Department of Homeland Security)

With the creation of the National Security Agency (NSA) in 1952, most joint military intelligence efforts relocated to Fort Meade, Maryland. Some elements stayed where they were, however. The annex was renamed as the Naval Security Station and, later in 1998, as the Nebraska Avenue Complex.

Naval Security Station, looking east from Nebraska Ave.
(Department of Homeland Security)

refurbished police call box featuring
WAVES decoder Alvina Schwab Pettigrew

The Department of Homeland Security established itself at the Nebraska Avenue Complex in January, 2003, two months after the department was created (integrating parts of 22 different federal departments and agencies). The Navy vacated the complex in 2005, but an anchor remains at the front as a memorial.

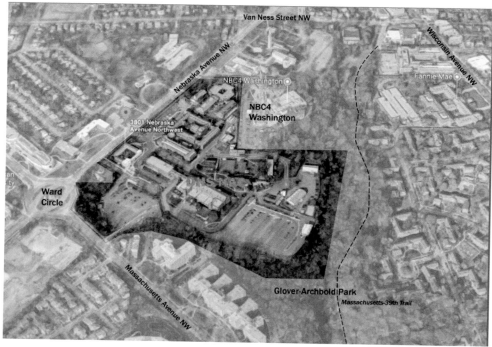

Department of Homeland Security, 2017 (National Capital Planning Commission)

65. Bright Young Spy

Victor Perlo, who lived at 4517 Brandywine Street in American University Park, was an economist who worked in several government agencies in the 1930s and 1940s. He was considered to be one of "Harry Hopkins' bright young men." The group helped create and implement a number of New Deal projects, including the Works Progress Administration (WPA) jobs program, unemployment compensation, the Wagner National Labor Relations Act, the Fair Labor Standards Act, and Social Security. After his government service ended in 1947, he worked as an economist for the Progressive Party, assisted the 1948 presidential campaign of Henry Wallace, became an economic consultant and university lecturer, and wrote 13 books.

In his private life, Perlo was a longtime member of the governing National Committee of the Communist Party USA. He was also a spy with the codename "Raider," according to decrypted Soviet cables. The ring he allegedly led supplied the USSR with economic, political, and military intelligence, including US aircraft production figures.

4517 Brandywine St. NW,
home of Soviet agent Victor Perlo

Perlo's secret was first revealed by his estranged wife, Katherine, after their divorce in 1943 and bitter child custody battle. In April 1944, Katherine wrote to President Franklin Roosevelt naming her husband and several members of his group as Soviet spies. None were arrested, however. Historian Kathryn Olmstead posits: "Possibly, the men of the FBI discounted the tale of an unstable, vengeful ex-wife. Or perhaps the tale of Russian espionage did not seem so sinister in 1944, when the brave Soviet allies were battling the Nazis. In any event, Katherine Perlo failed in her quest to destroy her ex-husband."

The next year, Perlo was fingered for a second time, now by fellow communist turned FBI informant Elizabeth Bentley. She said Perlo ran a spy network of several other federal officials, one of whom worked in the Office of Strategic Services (OSS, forerunner of the CIA). The FBI called the network the Perlo group because he was the undisputed leader. But Bentley had little evidence to back up her accusations and for decades Perlo and his supporters successfully contested the claim.

Repeatedly called to testify before congressional committees, Perlo was argumentative. Denying espionage, he said: "The dragging of my name through the mud is part of a big Roman circus." Even though confessed Soviet spy Whittaker Chambers also testified against him, Perlo's culpability was in doubt until release in the 1990s of Soviet cables decrypted under the Venona project run by the US Army's Signal Intelligence Service (later subsumed by the National Security Agency). This was the counter-intelligence effort that also seemed to prove the betrayal of US secrets to the USSR by Julius and Ethel Rosenberg, Klaus Fuchs, Alger Hiss, and Harry Dexter White. The latter, a senior Treasury department official who created the foundations of the World Bank and the International Monetary Fund, lived at The Westchester (*story 36*).

Perlo maintained his innocence to the end. He did not hide his admiration for the Soviet Union, to which he had both ideological and ancestral ties. His parents were Russian Jews who fled the Russian empire in their youth. Perlo joined the Communist Party while a student at Columbia University. He was described as a dogmatic Leninist who distained "fuzzy-minded liberals" whose promotion of inadequate reforms delayed the inevitable time when workers would seize power, as he saw it. After the Soviet Union collapsed in 1994, Perlo denounced Mikhail Gorbachev's "opportunistic petty-bourgeois capitulation to capitalism" and pined for the days of Stalinist order. None of this alone makes him a traitor, of course, and one must be wary of attempts by the FBI under long-time director J. Edgar Hoover to persecute leftists. But Soviet intelligence cables intercepted by the Venona project provide damning evidence. After Bentley's defection, the Soviet Secret Police, KGB, ordered its chief of operations in Washington, Anatoly Gorsky, to cease meeting with Perlo, among others. Gorsky also had to stop seeing British agent Donald Maclean, whom we will meet in the next story.

Assuming Perlo was a spy, the question is why? Most of those who spied for the Soviet Union did so for ideological reasons. They were idealistic, self-righteous, and impressionable. Perlo, in particular, was appalled by the Great Depression-era ravages of capitalism, by domestic racism, and by US foreign interventions in Latin America. In addressing the question of why he and others spied, Olmstead quotes another American who spied for the Soviet Union, physicist Theodore Hall, who said: "If you care very much for the well-being of the people of your country and you take a step with the intention of keeping them from a horrible catastrophe, that is not disloyalty. The experience of Auschwitz and the Gulag and Vietnam remind us that blind obedience to authority is not always a good kind of loyalty." America's wartime alliance with the Soviets provided another justification for espionage. Yet, Perlo and others continued their misguided loyalty long after the totalitarian nature of Soviet communism was crystal clear.

```
From:  WASHINGTON
To:    MOSCOW
No:    3713-3715                        29 June 1945

To the 8th Department.  Material from "RAIDER [REJDER]".[i]

     I am sending information extracted from the secret
program of the "JOINT AIRCRAFT COMMITTEE" of the "DEPOT"[ii]
of 25 May of this year concerning aircraft construction planned
for 1945-1946.

     In the first column is given the figure for the aircraft
construction planned for April-December 1945; in the second
column is the analogous figure for the whole of 1946.

     1. Four engine heavy bomber long range for the
        USAAF [AVVS] type-B-29:
```

extract from cable decrypted by the National Security Agency's Venona Project and transcribed by students of the Mercyhurst College Institute for Intelligence Studies (Wilson Center)

66.   British Traitors

The Tenleytown Heritage Trail leaves out what I consider to be the most interesting story of the neighborhood. In September 1949, debonair British diplomat Harold Adrian Russell Philby, who went by the nickname Kim, arrived in Washington with his family to take up his posting as First Secretary. During his two-year tenure, they lived at a five-bedroom tan brick colonial at 4100 Nebraska Avenue.

4100 Nebraska Ave, home of Kim Philby, 1949–1951

Kim Philby (1912–1988)
(1955; public domain)

Philby's real job was Secret Intelligence Service (MI6) station chief at the British Embassy, liaison officer to the FBI, and to the newly established CIA. He was also a double agent for the Soviet Union, the most notorious of the infamous "Cambridge Five." The top-secret US information that Philby gave his Soviet handlers resulted in the deaths of many brave men and women behind the Iron Curtain. Taking up residence in his basement was another of the five: Guy Burgess, an unstable alcoholic who also had a cover job at the British Embassy as information officer.

In his book *A Spy Among Friends,* Ben Macintyre tells the story of the "dinner party from hell" that Philby and his wife hosted at home for his senior contacts in American intelligence. At the end of a boozy meal, Burgess burst in "disheveled, loudly inebriated, and itching for a fight." When Libby Harvey, the high-strung wife of the man in charge of CIA counter-intelligence, drunkenly demanded that Burgess, known for his caricatures, sketched her, he did so as outrageously as possible. In his cartoon, "her dress was hiked up around her waist, her legs spread, and her naked pudenda bared." Uproar ensued.

A third member of the ring, Donald Maclean, was stationed in Washington a few years earlier. Codenamed "Homer," Maclean was Secretary of the Combined Policy Committee on atomic energy matters. Among the secrets he passed was the relatively small amount of plutonium

Donald Maclean (1913–1983) (public domain)

Guy Burgess (1911–1963) (1951, UK National Archives)

that was used in the "Fat Man" bomb dropped on Nagasaki. This intelligence gave the USSR the ability to determine the size of the US nuclear arsenal.

Maclean came under suspicion in 1951 due to intercepted cables by the Venona counter-intelligence project by the US Army's Signal Intelligence Service, to which Philby was privy. In May 1951, Burgess was sent back to London for bad behavior. In a single day, he had acquired three speeding tickets, insulted the arresting officers, and asserted diplomatic immunity. Philby later claimed he had arranged Burgess' de facto persona non grata status to get him to London in time to warn Maclean that he was about to be interrogated. Burgess relayed the warning but then disobeyed Philby's orders and escaped to Moscow along with Maclean.

Kim Philby on USSR stamp
(public domain)

The double disappearance caused an uproar at the British Embassy and put Philby in a tight spot, since he had been together with both of them at Cambridge and had hosted Burgess for many months. Worried that he himself might be placed under US surveillance, Philby left work early when the disappearance was discovered, saying he was going home for a stiff drink, as Macintyre relates. Back at 4100 Nebraska Avenue, Philby headed not for the liquor cabinet but for the shed in back to collect a trowel. Then from a hiding place in the basement of the house he retrieved tools of his traitorship — a Russian camera, tripod, and film — which he sealed in a waterproof container and put in the trunk of his car. He then drove off to a wooded stretch of the road near Old Angler's Inn in Great Falls, Maryland and buried the incriminating equipment between the road and the Potomac River. It has never been found.

Rather than then joining his fellow spies in exile, Philby bluffed it out for another decade and more. Although he came under suspicion by the counter-intelligence MI5, the upper crust in MI6 refused to believe that one of their own could turn traitor. He was the inspiration for the traitor hunted by George Smiley in John le Carré's *Tinker Tailor Soldier Spy*. Philby wasn't unmasked until 1963, at which point he also fled to the USSR, living there until he died in 1988. Moscow gave him a hero's funeral.

Thirty years after the traitor's death, best-selling author Daniel Silva recast part of the story through the tale of Philby's fictional daughter. Like him, Rebecca Manning, anti-heroine of the spy novel *The Other Woman*, was MI6 station chief in Washington while working as a double agent for masters in Moscow. Silva had her living on Warren Street, a couple blocks away from 4100 Nebraska Avenue, across from a communal green garden. By coincidence, my wife and I live on Warren Street, across from a communal green garden, although we do not have a flagstone walkway with an iron lamp like Manning had. In the novel, when her cover is blown and she hurriedly must flee to Dulles airport, she first stops near the Potomac in Great Falls, Maryland with a shovel to dig up her father's buried camera for sentimental sake.

67.   Tripped up by Overbilling

Stewart Nozette is a brainy aerospace scientist who conceived and led the mission of the Clementine spacecraft which in 1995 discovered evidence of water on the south side of the moon (a contested finding). Holding special access security clearances, he worked for a Department of Energy nuclear laboratory and the Department of Defense's Defense Advanced Research Projects Agency. These days, he is finishing out a 13-year sentence at the Federal Correctional Institution in Terre Haute, Indiana, for espionage and fraud, having sought to sell American nuclear and space technology to Israel.

Stewart Nozette, 2008 (NASA)

His story belongs in this book because Nozette lived just north of Friendship Heights, at 141 Grafton Street, Chevy Chase, Maryland.

141 Grafton St., Chevy Chase

Even before he left government work in 2006, Nozette ran a nonprofit corporation called Alliance for Competitive Technology, which he used for contracting with NASA and as a cash cow to cover personal expenses. In 2006, an inspector for the space agency found that he had overbilled NASA for a quarter-million dollars for expenses including three mortgages, nine credit cards, a tennis club, pool cleaning, and a sedan service. When the "nonprofit" organization did not comply with a request for bank records, federal agents raided his house. There they found a 2002 email in which Nozette threatened to take a classified program on which he was working to Israel or another country. The other country was not specified in court documents, but it likely was India, given that Nozette was heavily involved in India's extraterrestrial moon probe. Nozette also worked as a technical consultant for Israel Aerospace Industries, earning $225,000 on which he failed to pay US taxes.

The FBI then launched a separate investigation of Nozette over potential espionage. The feds were watching in January 2009 when he flew to India with two memory sticks, returning three weeks later without them. Two days later, he pleaded guilty to two counts of conspiracy to defraud the government and to tax evasion, promising to pay $265,205 in restitution to the government. Facing a possible two-year prison term, he told a colleague that if sentenced to jail he would flee to Israel, India, or Canada and "tell them everything" he knew. There is no public evidence that any of these countries engaged Nozette in espionage.

FBI surveillance video of Nozette talking to pretend Mossad agent at Mayflower Hotel (obtained under FOIA and released by the (Institute for Research: Middle Eastern Policy)

Anticipating that he might indeed flee, the FBI set up a sting operation two months before the sentencing date for the tax fraud and evasion trial. In September 2009, an FBI agent posing as an Israeli intelligence officer called Nozette and set up a meeting at the Mayflower Hotel in Washington. Nozette told the bogus Mossad agent of his espionage plans and said, "I knew this day would come. ...I knew you guys would show up. ...I thought I was working for you already." Over the next few weeks, FBI agents gave him cash in exchange for information he provided on a classified satellite, weapons-system research, and other secret national security matters. Saying the US government had invested $1 billion to develop the classified program he was sharing, Nozette asked for $2 million in compensation. As a down payment, the agent handed over $10,000. After Nozette pocketed it, the FBI busted him in the hotel.

The day of the arrest, next-door-neighbor Betty O'Connor said reporters asked her "How do you feel about having a spy in the neighborhood?" She replied, "How would you feel?" She added, "everyone knows it as the spy house."

68. Spying for Castro

Gwen and Kendall Myers, who lived at the Westchester *(story 36)*, were from Washington's social elite. Gwen had been an aide to Senator James Abourezk from her native state of South Dakota. They lived the good life, much of it aboard their $350,000 yacht. Kendall was a great-grandson of Alexander Graham Bell and grandson of Gilbert Grosvenor, longtime editor of *National Geographic*. Kendall was also related to President William Howard Taft. Until retiring in 2007, he worked at the State Department as a European analyst in the Bureau of Intelligence and Research, with access to top secret documents from across the US intelligence community.

Federal prosecutors wrote: "Unlike many defendants who appear for sentencing before this Court, Kendall Myers was born into this world with every conceivable advantage. …his was a life of wealth and privilege. He attended the finest schools, including a private boarding secondary school in Pennsylvania and Brown University for college. He also earned a Ph.D. from Johns Hopkins University. Kendall Myers could have been anything he wanted to be. He chose to be a Cuban spy.

"He chose to use his substantial intellect and education to prey on the most sensitive secrets of the United States. He took a federal oath of office "to support and defend the Constitution of the United States against all enemies foreign and domestic" that he never had any intention of honoring. He then sought and obtained jobs within the Department of State solely because they would give him the widest possible access to classified information that he could steal for CuIS [Cuban Intelligence Service]. He also developed friendships with other unwitting intelligence analysts just so he could exploit them for the benefit of Fidel Castro."

Kendall and Gwen Myers in Feb. 2009 (US government)

In 2010, the two were convicted of spying for Cuba for nearly 30 years. Kendall was sentenced to life imprisonment without parole; Gwen received seven years and died not long after her release. They spied not for money, but for ideology. They were liberals gone bad who, blind to its human rights abuses, became fixated on the idea that Castro's Cuba was a socialist nirvana. Spying became central to their relationship, as they reinforced each other's unwavering devotion to the revolution. His codename was "agent 123," hers were "agent 203" and "Agent E-63." One friend said, "Maybe Gwen is the one who had the thing for Cuba and he loved her so much he did it."

Before their sentencing in 2010, friends and relatives flooded the court with letters asking for leniency. Kendall's brother said Gwen and her husband "care deeply about people born into poverty and hopelessness." A friend wrote that Gwen Myers had the "unassuming, unpretentious honesty that's completely typical of the upper Midwest."

Kendall seemed to have had a midlife crisis after he hit and killed a teenager at a time when he was divorcing his first wife. He started working for Cuba in 1979 after a two-week visit there at the invitation of a Cuban agent he had met at a Georgetown soiree. At the time, Kendall was working in an unclassified job at the State Department's Foreign Service Institute (FSI). (This was the year that I joined the State Department and was myself attending classes at FSI.) Later, he applied for an intelligence position at the State Department at the suggestion of CuIS.

At times, the couple passed information to their Cuban handlers at the Giant Food supermarket at Wisconsin Avenue and Newark Street and other grocery stores by exchanging shopping carts. This required letting the other side know beforehand what groceries they wanted.

The couple was caught after a tip by a US asset in Cuba and a three-year investigation during which their apartment at the Westchester was bugged. An FBI search of their quarters turned up a radio they used to receive

Giant Food at Wisconsin and Newark

instructions, but no classified documents. Circumstantial evidence, however, included a sailing guide to Cuban waters, a book entitled *On Becoming Cuban* by Louis A. Pérez, Jr. and *The Spy's Bedside Book* by Graham Greene.

(Federal Bureau of Investigation)

Kendall Myers was not the only government official convicted of spying for Castro. Nine years earlier, a senior analyst at the Defense Intelligence Agency (DIA), Ana Belén Montes, was arrested and sentenced to 25 years in prison for the same crime. Montes seemed like an unlikely traitor. Nicknamed the "Queen of Cuba" by her DIA colleagues for her superlative research on that country, she had a sister and brother employed by the FBI. But she was known to disagree with US policy toward Latin America and her first contact with handlers was made when she attended the Johns Hopkins School of Advanced International Studies in 1983–1984. She lived in an apartment at 3039 Macomb Street in Cleveland Park.

Then there was the stunning South African blonde Jennifer Miles *(right)*. While working in the South African Embassy in the late 1960s, she became a Cuban asset, codenamed "Mary." The FBI saw she was entertaining officials at her apartment at 2800 Wisconsin Avenue, and arrested her after she began engaging White House staffers. She was then deported, under curious circumstances that made some people assume she was a South African double agent.

Jennifer Miles with Cuban handler Rogelio Rodriguez López, mid-1969 (FBI surveillance photo)

69.   Sleeper Agent

Remember the ten Russian agents arrested in 2010 whose stories became the basis of the acclaimed TV show *The Americans*? One of them lived in the DC area and sometimes contacted his Russian handler at the intersection of Wisconsin Avenue and Van Ness Street. Sitting in the Tenleytown Ruby Tuesday (now Surfside), 28-year old Mikhail Semenko transmitted encrypted messages wirelessly from his laptop to a Russian "diplomat" parked in the McDonald's lot across the street. Who would guess that this nondescript corner was the site of such intrigue?

Mikhail Semenko outside the White House (from social media site Odnoklassniki)

Semenko transmitted wireless messages from Ruby Tuesday (now Surfside) to his handler in the parking lot at McDonald's

Semenko, who speaks five languages, had come to the United States five years earlier for a master's degree at Seton Hall University in New Jersey. He got a job at a Russian travel agency in Arlington, drove a beat-up 1992 Toyota Camry, was active on social media, and set about trying to fulfill his mission. The federal complaint against him and another agent said their long-term mission on behalf of the Russian foreign intelligence organ "SVR"(successor to the KGB) was "to become sufficiently 'Americanized' such that they can gather information about the United States for Russia, and can successfully recruit sources who are in, or are able to infiltrate, United States policy-making circles." In other words, he was a sleeper agent, working under deep cover. The Russian intelligence services called such agents "illegals," meaning they had no diplomatic protection.

Semenko was the youngest of the ten sleeper agents arrested in 2010, and one of the only two to be single and to use his real name. Most of the others were sent by the SVR under the guise of married couples. Most came via Canada where they acquired backstories by taking on the names of deceased Canadian citizens. Several had children who, like in the TV series, did not know their parents' real identity until the arrests. Another sad part of the story is that the children had to move to Russia without knowing the language or considering it home.

Semenko was the only one who lived in the capital area; the others had suburban homes in New Jersey, Manhattan, Yonkers, and Boston. The other unmarried one was the engaging young Anna Chapman. After returning to Russia, she launched a successful career in television hosting and modeling and wrote social media posts supportive of President Donald Trump.

US counter-intelligence officials learned about the spy ring thanks to a disillusioned SRV mole named Alexander Poteyev and the cracking of a secret code. The sleeper agents were surveilled for several years under the FBI's Operation Ghost Stories investigation and not arrested until one of them was getting chummy with a senior official. British tabloids claimed that Chapman had come perilously close to seducing a member of President Barack Obama's cabinet and that was why the FBI swooped in when it did. However, the FBI said such claims were patently false and that the real impetus for the arrests was because another of the ten had been in close business contact with a friend of then-Secretary of State Hillary Clinton. All ten pleaded guilty to secretly acting as agents of the Russian government. None of them were actually charged with espionage because they had failed to pass along any classified information.

Two weeks after the arrests, the ten Russian agents were flown to Vienna Airport. Like in the days of the Cold War, they were exchanged on the tarmac for four individuals whom Russia had arrested on grounds of spying for the West. When asked by *Tonight Show* host Jay Leno why the United States was seemingly short-changed on the deal, then-Vice President Joe Biden joked that the ten Russians arrested were not the most adept of spies. "We got back four really good ones," Biden said.

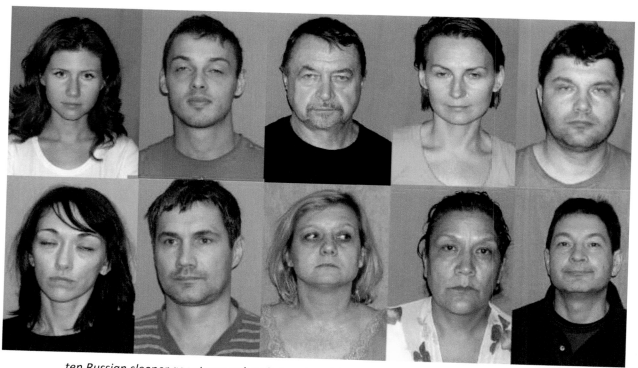

ten Russian sleeper agents apprehended on June 27, 2010; Anna Chapman pictured upper left
(US Marshals Service)

One of the four traded by Moscow was Sergei Skripal, who had worked for Russian military intelligence (GRU) and spied for Britain's MI6. Eight years after he began a new life in Salisbury, England, the GRU sent two assassins to his home, poisoning him and his daughter Yulia with a Novichok nerve agent and inadvertently killing two British citizens who had picked up the discarded perfume bottle in which the assassins had kept the nerve agent.

Yulia and Sergei Skripal survived nerve agent poisoning in 2018 (Julia Skripal: Facebook)

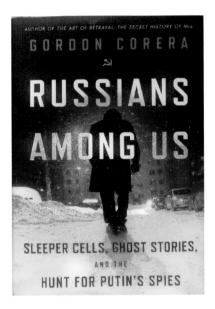

Experts believe that Russia is still running sleeper agents in the United States as one element of its ramped-up intelligence gathering and influence operations. There is debate about the usefulness of such operations and their cost effectiveness. The FBI estimates the sleeper program cost $50 million, some of which was passed to the agents in classic Cold War tradecraft methods such as exchanging bags in the subway. A friend of mine at the BBC, Gordon Corera, published a lively book in 2020 about the FBI investigation. He argues that the longer-term penetration of the illegals posed a genuine threat and demonstrated Russia's persistence and patience in targeting its adversary. "Illegals are the pride of Soviet and then Russian intelligence," Corera concludes.

70. Russian Redhead

On July 15, 2018, six FBI agents descended on an apartment in McLean Gardens on Wisconsin Avenue *(story 17)*. Inside, a stylish 29-year-old Russian woman and her 57-year-old boyfriend were packing up to move to his home in Sioux Falls, South Dakota.

The spying accusations against Maria Butina seemed damning. Her relationship with Paul Erickson, the bald Republican political operative twice her age, was merely a "necessary aspect of her activities," the Justice Department initially claimed. Her pursuit of a master's degree at American University was a cover, prosecutors once said. They also originally said she was willing to offer sex in order to infiltrate conservative organizations such as the National Rifle Association. She allegedly was working at the behest of a Russian central banker. The imminent move to the hinterland also looked suspicious. The press lapped the story up.

Maria Butina, Dec 19, 2014
(Pavel Starikov: Wikipedia Commons)

Maria Butina lived at 3617 38th St.
in McLean Gardens

But the FBI's seven-hour search of Butina's apartment turned up nothing incriminating. Ditto the surveillance of her beforehand. Finding no evidence that she had received money or instructions from the Russian government, the prosecutors dropped many of their initial accusations. They did not press charges against Erickson or any other Americans allegedly involved in her scheme (although Erickson was indicted on wire fraud and money laundering charges in a separate case in South Dakota). Alexander Torshin, the Russian central banker with whom she communicated and sought "orders," was a fellow gun enthusiast. Prosecutors eventually admitted that she was not a spy in the traditional sense, nor could they make a case that she was a sleeper agent, like the ten Russians discussed in the preceding story.

Prosecutors did successfully charge Butina with conspiracy to act as an unregistered agent of Russia, under a law enacted in 1948 during the "Red Scare" days of Joseph McCarthy. She pleaded guilty to trying to infiltrate conservative political circles and promote Russian interests before and after the 2016 presidential election. The judge said Butina's work on behalf of Russia was "sophisticated and penetrated deep into political organizations." She was the first Russian citizen convicted of crimes relating to the election, although her efforts seem to have been independent of the Kremlin's sweeping election interference. Butina was more of a pawn in a Russian influence campaign in which Torshin was a player. He had been building up contacts on the

Maria Butina after arrest on July 15, 2018 (Alexandria Detention Center mug shot)

right of American politics for several years. While Butina's contact with him involved "taskings" of the kind that agents receive, there was no sign of clandestine communications.

BBC reporter Gordon Corera concludes that Butina was not a spy in the traditional sense, nor even a "special agent" illegal like Anna Chapman. Rather, her overt work was an example of how Russian influence activities have continued to evolve. Even if not an actual spy, she was providing information to Moscow about Americans with political influence who might be susceptible to recruitment. "Russian spying was becoming more opportunistic," Corera writes. Quasi-agents like Butina provide more plausible deniability and are disposable, in that they are not trained officers with secrets in their head who need to be retrieved or swapped if caught.

After 15 months in jail, Butina was released in November 2019 and deported to Russia, returning to her hometown in remote Siberia. Shortly afterwards, the Russian Commissioner for Human Rights offered Butina a job working on behalf of Russians imprisoned abroad. There has been little news in the English press about her since then.

This is not the end of the story, however. After her arrest, Russian President Vladimir Putin suggested that it would lead to retribution. "The law of retaliation states, 'An eye for an eye or a tooth for a tooth,' " he said in a news conference. Eight days later, Russian authorities arrested Paul Nicholas Whelan, a former US Marine, and charged him with espionage. He had gone to Moscow to attend a wedding. Commentators suggested he was likely arrested in retaliation and with the idea of a trade. Yet after Butina was released, Whelan's detention period was extended. On June 15, 2020, after a secret trial, he was sentenced to 16 years in prison. The Russians apparently now want to swap him for a bigger fish.

Paul Whelan (provided by the family)

Epilogue

Once I began seriously exploring my neighborhood, I was amazed at how much history I was able to uncover while stretching my legs. Being comparatively young, Washington, DC cannot compete with the centuries of lore offered by London, the last city that I called home. But in terms of interesting stories per square mile, I doubt that any locale in the Western Hemisphere, save New York City, can beat our nation's capital.

I trust that the preceding pages have conveyed a bit of the love I feel for the city. Washington often gets a bum rap, especially by politicians from the rest of the country who use DC as a verbal punching bag. Granted, Washington is far from perfect. Those who live here like to complain about our lack of political representation in Congress and more mundane matters like potholes and tree maintenance. Yet we are generally satisfied. And why not? Residing at the center of the political universe has many advantages. We may not be in the room, but we live in the city where it happens.

The thousands of diplomats in our midst and the foreigners who work at institutions such as the World Bank and International Monetary Fund are neighbors who add spice and style to our surroundings. Ditto, dedicated public servants like Dr. Anthony Fauci whose house I saw on a recent walk. (I could tell it was his block, because it was the epicenter of yard signs that sprouted throughout the city in mid-2020 saying: "Thank you Dr. Fauci!") Washingtonians also benefit from proximity to the many buildings of the Smithsonian Institution and other museums and repositories of art and memorabilia. One does not even have to venture inside; DC is beautiful architecturally and botanically, especially in the northwest quadrant (in contrast to less-privileged areas in the eastern quadrants). Most importantly, from my perspective, history has its eyes on this place (to borrow again from Lin-Manuel Miranda). From the vantage point of my neighborhood, I hope readers also have learned how much Washington, DC has contributed to making America a great country, however imperfect it may be.

Acknowledgments

Writing this book about a village took a village. I am indebted to many neighbors, colleagues, friends, and relatives who helped and encouraged me along the way. In particular, fellow former Foreign Service Officer and neighborhood hiking enthusiast Jim Zumwalt and American University research librarian Kathryn Ray provided careful peer reviews, greatly improving the draft manuscript. Her colleague Katie Hut as well as Leslie Nellis from the AU archives staff promptly answered my inquiries. Rhoda Trooboff and Jane Waldmann were among several longtime residents of the area to share insights. Michele Casto and her colleagues at the Washingtoniana Special Collections section of the DC Public Library cheerfully answered my many photo requests. Lars-Erik Tindre from the Embassy of Sweden, and Bonnie Matheson, who grew up at UnderOak were among those generous with their time. Elizabeth Nottingham invited me into her Dunblane home. Kyle Hawke at Three Ocean Press provided vital copy editing.

I was also able to draw on help from a large network of friends. Jim O'Neal offered advice from his own publishing experience. Kevin Maher had useful thoughts on legal matters. Don Camp and Robert Hunt helped me get my facts right in areas of their expertise. Charles Walsh recommended the formula for the title, to which many others then suggested improvements. Scott Van Orsdel, Susan Burk, Mark Goodman, and Robin Prochazka were among the many friends who offered ongoing encouragement.

This book became a family enterprise in many ways. Tom Fitzpatrick made several helpful suggestions, including on topics relating to discrimination. Robbie Fitzpatrick lent his professional knowledge in the art field. Kristin (Kimball) Mishra shared experiences as a former Washingtonian. Julie Kramer had advice as a practiced author. Mike Fitzpatrick caught several numerical mistakes. Ann Page did a final proofread. Katie (Fitzpatrick) Lawrence coached me on formatting, design, and printing. Many other relatives cheered me along. My patient wife, Kyoko, offered careful editing at several stages, invaluable judgment, and, most importantly, loving support. Having had no stronger backers than my parents, I regret that my father left this world in August before he could see the final product.

Notes

URLs accessed October 12, 2020.

Introduction: Matt Johnson, "Washington's systematic streets," Greater Greater Washington, August 7, 2009; Judith Beck Helm, *Tenleytown, D.C.: Country Village into City Neighborhood* (1981); Cultural Tourism DC, "Top of the Town: Tenleytown Heritage Trail" (2010), https://www.culturaltourismdc.org/portal/829.

1. Indigenous quarries: Helm, *Tenleytown, D.C.*, p. 3; Wayne Henry Holmes, *Stone Implements of the Potomac-Chesapeake-Tidewater Province* (1897), pp. 108, 119, 122-124; Ann Kessler, "Lost Forest Hills: The Rose Hill Quarry," *Forest Hills Connection*, December 12, 2019.

2. Tenleytown: Helm, *Tenleytown, D.C.*, pp. 40-45. 104, 139; BBC "When Charles Dickens fell out with America," February 14, 2012.

3. Boundary Marker: Lin-Manuel Miranda, *Hamilton: An American Musical* (2015); "Boundary Stones of the District of Columbia," https://boundarystones.org/.

4. Coaches: Helm, *Tenleytown, D.C.*, pp. 57-58, 232-238, 566-570; Metro platform photo by Swagging, https://commons.wikimedia.org /wiki/File:Tenleytown-AU_station.jpg; "History," Washington Metropolitan Area Transit Authority, https://www.wmata.com/about/history.cfm.

5. Dumblane: Helm, *Tenleytown, D.C.*, pp. 88, 226-230, 388, 390, 493; "Dumblane: A Southern Craftsman Home," *The Craftsman*, February 1913; Gadi Dechter "Robinson Nottingham," *Baltimore Sun*, May 26, 2008; communication with Elizabeth Nottingham, October 2020; Daniel Burke, "The lavish homes of American archbishops," *CNN*, August 2014.

6. Fort Bayard: "Civil War Defenses of Washington," National Park Service, https://www.nps.gov/cwdw/index.htm.

7. Fort Gaines: Helm, *Tenleytown, D.C.*, pp. 116-117; Robert Lebling, "America's Zouaves," *AramcoWorld*, March/April 2017.

8. Fort Reno: Helm, *Tenleytown, D.C.*, pp. 152-158; Neil Flanagan, "The Battle of Fort Reno," *Washington City Paper*, November 2, 2017.

9. Erased Community: Helm, *Tenleytown, D.C.*, pp. 199-203; Flanagan, "The Battle of Fort Reno;" "Designated Historic Sites," Tenleytown Historical Society; Scott Beyer, "How the U.S. Government Destroyed Black Neighborhoods," *Catalyst*, April 2, 2020; Alejandra Matos, "The District's most coveted middle school is losing its principal," *Washington Post*, June 7, 2017.

10. James Wormley: Cultural Tourism DC, "African American Heritage Trail (2003); Donald D. Graves, "Wormley Hotel," White House Historical Association; Nicholas E. Hollis, "A Hotel for the History Books," *Washington Post*, March 18, 2001.

11. Call Boxes: Richard Scarry, *Busiest Fire Fighters Ever!*, (A Little Golden Book, 1993), p. 12; H.A. Rey, *Curious George* (1941), p. 33; "Art on Call," Cultural Tourism DC.

12. Friendship Heights: Helm, *Tenleytown, D.C.*, pp. 14, 369; Yasda Khademian, "Ten Facts You May Not Know About Friendship Heights," *dcist*, October 7, 2019.

13. National Cathedral: Washington National Cathedral, https://cathedral.org/; Bob Woodward, *Rage* (2020), pp. 71-74; "Two Cathedrals," The West Wing: Second Season, written by Aaron Sorkin, directed by Thomas Schlamme, NBC, May 16, 2001; communication with Kevin Eckstrom, Chief Communications Officer, National Cathedral, September 2020.

14. **National Bureau of Standards**: Michael Lewis, *The Fifth Risk: Undoing Democracy* (2018). p. 159; John DeFerrari, "The Lost Hilltop Home of The National Bureau of Standards," *Streets of Washington*, July 1, 2013; *National Geographic*, "A Wonderland of Science," February 1915.

15. **Fire Station!**: Cultural Tourism DC, "Top of the Town."

16. **Masonic Temple**: "William R. Singleton-Hope-Lebanon Lodge #7," https://www.singletonlodge.com/; "The Grand Lodge of D.C.: Freemasonry in the Nation's Capital," https://www.dcgrandlodge.org/; Robert L.D. Cooper, *Cracking the Freemason's Code* (2006), pp.1, 16, 79, 192, 203; Elaine Paulionis Phelen, "Mozart's Masonic Opera: The Magic Flute," The Masonic Philosophical Society, November 9, 2015.

17. **McLean Gardens**: "History," McLean Gardens, http://www.mcleangardens.com/home.asp; "Why is it Named McLean Gardens?" *Ghosts of DC*, October 16, 2013; Carl Sferranza Anthony, *Florence Harding: The First Lady, The Jazz Age, and the Death of America's Most Scandalous President (1998)*, p. 133; Kathryn Smith, *The Gatekeeper* (2016), p. 151; Chalmers M. Roberts, "Uncovering a Coverup on Teapot Dome," *Washington Post*, June 9, 1977; "History of the Hope Diamond," Smithsonian, https://www.si.edu/spotlight/hope-diamond/history.

18. **American Creed**: Helm, *Tenleytown, D.C*, p. 338-339; Gunner Myrdal, *An American dilemma: The negro problem and modern democracy* (1944), p. 3; *American Creed*, directed by Sam Ball, Citizen Film and WTTW Chicago for PBS (2017), https://www.americancreed.org/.

19. **American University**: "History," American University, https://www.american.edu/about/history.cfm; George E. Lowe, "The Camelot Affair," *Bulletin of the Atomic Scientists*, Vol. 22, No. 5 (May 1966).

20. **'Merica**: "How to Say America in Different Languages," In Different Languages, https://www.indifferentlanguages.com/words/america.

21. **Ward Circle**: Patrick Bradley, "Artemas Ward: AU's Second Cousin, Completely Removed," American University September 8, 2011, https://www.american.edu/ocl/news/who-is-artemas-ward.cfm; "General Ward," General Artemas Ward House Museum, Harvard University, https://wardhouse.harvard.edu/general-ward; "Kin of Revolution Hero Unveils Statue," *Washington Herald*, November 4, 1938.

22. **American University Law School**: "History," American University Washington College of Law, https://www.wcl.american.edu/impact/history/, Helm, *Tenleytown, D.C.*, p. 247.

23. **John F. Kennedy Speech Plaza**: President John F. Kennedy, "Commencement Address at American University, Washington, D.C.," June 10, 1963, John F. Kennedy Presidential library and Museum, https://www.jfklibrary.org/archives/other-resources/john-f-kennedy-speeches/american-university-19630610; Tibor Tóth, "Building Up the Regime for Verifying the CTBT," *Arms Control Today*, September 2009; "The Nuclear Testing Tally; Fact sheets and briefs," Arms Control Association, July 2020; https://www.armscontrol.org/factsheets/nucleartesttally.

24. **Easter Island Statue**: "Easter Island statue given to AU," *American Neighborhood*, Summer/Fall 2000; "Easter Island statue, first of many to enrich campus," *American magazine*, summer 2000; "Easter Island History," Chile Culture, http://www.chileculture.org/easter-island-history/; Colin Casey, "Chilean President Dedicates New Mural at AU Museum," *American University News*, October 3, 2016.

25. **Korean Stone Grandfathers**: "American Univ. to open Korean garden with cherry trees," *Dong-A Ilbo*, April 20, 2011.

26. **Katzen Arts Center:** Jo Ann Lewis, "A Dentist Who Put Teeth In AU's Artistic Ambition," *Washington Post*, July 3, 2005; "Katzen Arts Center," American University, https://www.american.edu/cas/katzen/.

27. **World War I Camps**: Helm, *Tenleytown, D.C., pp. 413-415.* Martin K. Gordon, Barry R. Sude, et al, "A Brief History of the American University Experimental Station and U.S. Navy Bomb Disposal School, American University," prepared under the Defense Environmental Restoration Program for U.S. Army Engineer District,

Baltimore; Office of History Headquarters, U.S. Army Corps of Engineers, June 1994, https://www.nab.usace.army.mil/Portals/63/docs/SpringValley/AUES_Report_June_1994.pdf, pp. 15-19, 44-46.

28. Chemical Weapons Program: Elliot Carter, "American University Once Had A Chemical Warfare Center," *Architect of the Capital*, November 23, 2016.

29. Death Valley: Steve Vogel, "Search to Resume for WWI Chemicals," *Washington Post*, January 24, 1999; Jaffee, "Ground Zero"; "How to Be Uncertain; or, My Cold War Kitchen Cabinets," National Toxic Land/Labor Conservation Service, August 21, 2015; Weapons of Mass Destruction in DC, http://wmdindc.blogspot.com/.

30. Spring Valley: map by James Hare - Derived from File:DC neighborhoods map.png by Peter Fitzgerald; Leigh Giangreco, "10 Facts You May Not Know About Spring Valley," *dcist*, WAMU 88.5 American University Radio, January 11, 2019; "Senator Nixon Signs Restrictive Covenant," *Ghosts of DC*, July 24, 2012; "Ormes and the Man," *Time*, November 17, 1961; Benefsheh D. Verell, "Spring Valley, Washington DC: Changing Land Use and Demographics from 1900–2000," *The Geographical Bulletin by Gamma Theta Upsilon*, 49: 103-119 (2008); Robert Wallace and H. Keith Melton, *Spy Sites of Washington, DC: A guide to the capital region's secret history* (2017), p 205

31. Convent of Bon Secours: Cultural Tourism DC, "Top of the Town;" "History," Bon Secours, https://bonsecours.us/about/history/; "Our History," Yuma Center, https://www.yumadc.org/history.

32. UnderOak: Helm: *Tenleytown, D.C.*, pp. 491-493; Donna Evers, "Inside Homes: Great Estates," *Washington Life*, January 20, 2012; "Deb of the Year," *Town & Country,* June 1962; Sean Wilsey, *Oh the Glory of it All* (2005) pp. 56-60; communication with Bonnie Matheson, October 2020.

33. Sidwell Friends: "About," Sidwell Friends, https://www.sidwell.edu/about; Adam Harris, "Parents Gone Wild: High Drama Inside D.C.'s Most Elite Private School," *The Atlantic*, June 5, 2019; communications with Kristin Mishra, May and August 2020; Jackson Knapp, "Sidwell Friends School Was Protested in Attempt to Save Nearby Elder-Care Facility," *Washingtonian*, April 29, 2016; "Sidwell delaying North Cleveland Park expansion; Murch renovation on schedule," *Forest Hills Connection*, August 2, 2017.

34. Van Ness Reservoir: John Kelly, "Answer Man Taps Into His High-Pressure Sources," *Washington Post*, May 20, 2007; D.W. Rowlands, "The fascinating story of DC's aqueducts and reservoirs," Greater Greater Washington, July 23, 2008; Larry Van Dyne, "Water, Water…," *Washingtonian*, March 1, 2007.

35. Alban Towers: Catherine Finn, "Looking back: Alban Towers," *dcdist*, April 24, 2011; Daniela Deane, "Alban Towers' Pricey, Historic Address," *Washington Post*, May 12, 2001; James M. Goode. *Best Addresses: A Century of Washington's Distinguished Apartment Houses* (1988); Wallace and Melton, *Spy Sites of Washington, DC*, pp. 68-69.

36. The Westchester: Amanda Abrams, "Where We Live: The Westchester, a D.C. building of a different era," *Washington Post*, December 6, 2011; "Oral History Interview with Mike Mansfield," Oral History Number: 391-010, ScholarWorks, September 9, 1999; communications with Jim Zumwalt, July, August, 2020.

37. Wagshal's Deli: Giangreco, "10 Facts You May Not Know About Spring Valley"; "Our Story," Wagshal's, https://www.wagshals.com/our-story.

38. The Washington Ballet: "About the Washington Ballet," The Washington Ballet, https://www.washingtonballet.org/about/; Sarah L. Kaufman and Peggy McGlone, "Washington Ballet is struggling with empty seats and a $3 million debt. What will turn it around?" *Washington Post*, October 22, 2018; Sarah Kaufman, "Washington Ballet loses top executive, cancels 'The Nutcracker' and rest of 2020 season," *Washington Post*, July 30, 2020.

39. Victory Garden: "Friendship Community Garden: A hidden oasis," May 30, 2014, Tenleytown, D.C., https://tenleytowndc.org/2014/05/30/friendship-community-garden-a-hidden-oasis/; "DC Gardeners Oral History

Project — Rhoda Trooboff," October 3, 2013, DC Digital Museum, https://wdchumanities.org/dcdm/items/show/1768; communication with Rhoda Trooboff, May 2020.

40. Western Union Tower: "Designated Historic Sites," Tenleytown Historical Society; Cultural Tourism DC, "Top of the Town."

41. Gandhi and Monism: Gandhi Memorial Center, http://www.gandhimemorialcenter.org/; Jeffrey Gettleman, "Seventy-one years later, Gandhi's influence in India diminishes," *New York Times*, 30 January 2019; "Monism," The Basics of Philosophy, https://www.philosophybasics.com/branch_monism.html; Andrea Wulf, *The Invention of Nature: Alexander Von Humboldt's New World* (2015), p. 370.

42. Washington Hebrew Congregation: "About Us," Washington Hebrew Congregation, https://www.whctemple.org/about-us; Rachel Kurzius, " 'Hate-Filled' Graffiti Discovered At Washington Hebrew Congregation," *dcist*, October 21, 2019.

43. NBC Studio: Lisa Birkbeck, "An old coat and a ping pong ball = Kermit?" National Museum of American History, August 26, 2010; Giangreco, "10 Facts You May Not Know About Spring Valley;" Greg Botelho, "The day politics and TV changed forever," CNN, March 14, 2016; John Kelly, "John Kelly's Washington: Where was Grasslands?" *Washington Post*, December 17, 2011.

44. Home of the Gecko: "GEICO's Story from the Beginning," GEICO, https://www.geico.com/about/corporate/history-the-full-story/. Tim Nudd, "Why Geico's gecko is now a cockney yob," *AdWeek*, February 16, 2006.

45. Continuity of government: Elliot Carter, "Fort Reno's Continuity of Government Tower," Architect of the Capital: hidden history in Washington D.C., November 12, 2016; Clara Jeffery, "Slim Pickins," *Washington CityPaper*, January 20, 1995.

46. National Presbyterian Church: "History of National Presbyterian Church," https://nationalpres.org/our-story; Religion and Ethics NewsWeekly, "Obama Church Shopping," PBS, December 13, 2008; Sarah Pulliam Bailey, Julie Zauzmer and Josh Dawsey, "Trump mocks the faith of others. His own religious practices remain opaque," *Washington Post*, February 14, 2020.

47. Shroom House: Marisa M. Kashino, "Bethesda's Famous 'Mushroom House' is For Sale," *Washingtonian*, May 16, 2018. "Roy Mason, Obituary," *The Futurist*, September–October 1996; Cameron Luttrell, "Bethesda's 'Mushroom House' Hits the Market for $1.5M," *Washingtonian*, May 29, 2018.

48. Fannie Mae: Wendy Connett, "Fannie Mae: What It Does And How It Operates," Investopedia, March 18, 2020; J. Linn Allen, "Mortgage Bias Riles Fannie Mae," *Chicago Tribune*, August 31, 1992; Daniel J. Sernovitz, "Deal of the Year," *Washington Business Journal*, April 27, 2017.

49. Peter Muhlenberg: Joshua *Horn,* "Peter Muhlenberg: The Pastor Turned Soldier," *Journal of the American Revolution*, November 9, 2015.

50. Senator Feinstein's House: Mary K. Mewborn, "Real Estate News," *Washington Life Magazine*, October 2001; "Obama, Clinton hold talks in Feinstein's living room," CNN Politics, June 6, 2008; "More on the Obama-Clinton Meeting," *New York Times*, June 6, 2008.

51. #Pizzagate: Marc Fisher, John Woodrow Cox and Peter Hermann, "Pizzagate: From rumor, to hashtag, to gunfire in D.C.," *Washington Post*, December 6, 2016; Rachel Kurzius, "Man pleads guilty to arson at Comet Ping Pong," *dcist*, December 18, 2019; Ann Limpert, "Comet Ping Pong Has Been Getting a New Uptick in Pizzagate Messages," *Washingtonian*, May 11, 2020.

52. International Chancery Center: Nicholas Bonard, "The International Chancery Center — The First Foreign Mission Enclave," National Capital Planning Commission, June 25, 2018; "Foreign Missions Center Master Plan At

Former Walter Reed Army Medical Center," Department of State, December 2018, https://www.state.gov/wp-content/uploads/2019/05/FMC-Master-Plan-FINAL.pdf.

53. Israeli Embassy: Yeshaiau Mandel, "U.S.-Israel Relations: History of Israel's U.S. Embassy," Jewish Virtual Library; Wallace and Melton, *Spy Sites of Washington, DC,* p. 218-220; Sonia Moghe, "Convicted Israel spy Jonathan Pollard free after 30 years," CNN, November 20, 2015.

54. PRC Embassy: Larry Van Dyne, "Foreign Affairs: DC's Best Embassies," *Washingtonian*, February 1, 2008; Didi Kirsten Tatlow, "To: Chinese Embassy, United States; Address: No. 1 Liu Xiaobo Plaza," *New York Times*, June 25, 2014; Emma Batha, "U.N. urged to investigate organ harvesting in China," Reuters, September 24, 2019.

55. Representing Taiwan: "TECRO Profile and Mission," Taipei Economic and Cultural Representative Office in the United States, https://www.roc-taiwan.org/us_en/post/18.html; "Taiwan says it did not receive WHO meeting invite, issue off the table for now," Reuters, May 18, 2020; Bonnie S. Glaser and Michael J. Green, "What Is the U.S. 'One China' Policy, and Why Does it Matter?" Center for Strategic and International Studies, January 13, 2017.

56. Brazilian Army Commission: National Area Planning Commission report, Foreign Missions and International Organizations in Washington, D.C, June 2002; Brazilian Army Commission, http://www.cebw.org/en/; communication with Brazilian official, July 2020.

57. Russian Embassy: Kenneth Bredemeier, "Soviets Take the High Ground," *Washington Post*, June 16, 1985; Fenit Nirappil, "Street signs outside Russian embassy in Washington now honor slain dissident," *Washington Post*, February 27, 2018; John Kelly, "What lies beneath? FBI tunnel in Glover Park heated up the Cold War," *Washington Post*, February 27, 2016; Larry Van Dyne, "Foreign Affairs: DC's Best Embassies," *Washingtonian*, February 1, 2008.

58. Caribbean Integration: "About the OECS," Organisation of Eastern Caribbean States, https://www.oecs.org/who-we-are/about-us; "Who We Are," CARICOM Caribbean Community, https://caricom.org/our-community/who-we-are/; Ding Ding and Inci Otker, "Strengthening Caribbean Regional Integration," International Monetary Fund, February 4, 2020; Dennis Chung, "One from ten leaves nought," *Jamaica Observer*, February 05, 2016.

59. South Korea's residence: Gregg Jaffee, "Ground Zero," *Washingtonian*, December 2, 2000; "How to Be Uncertain;" communications with Kathleen Stephens and Kongdon (Katy) Oh, July, October 2020.

60. Japanese Ambassador's residence: Michael M. Clements, "Take a Look Inside the Residence of Japanese Ambassador Shinsuke J. Sugiyama," *Capitol File*, April 3, 2019.

61. Swedish Ambassador's residence: Fritz Hahn, "Hidden inside Washington's embassies: A world of fun (and free) stuff to do," *Washington Post,* November 28, 2018; Larry Van Dyne, "Foreign Affairs: DC's Best Embassies," *Washingtonian*, February 1, 2008; "Washington D.C, Ambassador's Residence," National Property Board of Sweden, https://www.sfv.se/fastigheter/sok/utrikes/nord-och-sydamerika/washington-d-c-ambassadorens-residens; Laura Snapes and AP, "Rapper A$AP Rocky charged with assault over fight in Sweden," *Guardian*, July 25, 2019; communication with Lars-Erik Tindre, head of public diplomacy for the Embassy of Sweden, October 2020.

62. Yemeni Ambassador's residence: "Prolonged conflict would make Yemen the poorest country in the world, UNDP study says," United Nations Development Program, September 26, 2019.

63. Mexican Ambassador's residence: Larry Luxner, "Mexico's Gerónimo Gutiérrez: Break Down Bilateral Walls, Don't Build Them," *The Washington Diplomat*, December 21, 2017; Deb Riechmann and Jill Colvin, "Trump forgoes insults of past, calls Mexico cherished friend," AP, July 8, 2020.

64. Code-busters: "History of the Nebraska Avenue Complex (NAC)," Department of Homeland Security, https://www.dhs.gov/history-nac."

65. Bright Young Spy: Wallace and Melton, *Spy Sites of Washington, DC*, p. 98; Kathryn S. Olmsted, *Red Spy Queen: A Biography of Elizabeth Bentley* (2002), pp. 54-56. 66-67, 102, 106; Hope Hale Davis, *Great Day Coming: A Memoir of the 1930s* (1994), p. 73; Victor Perlo, "Reply to Herbert Aptheker," *Political Affairs* (June 1992), pp. 25-29; John Earl Hayes, "Venona Project and Vassiliev Notebooks Index and Concordance," Wilson Center, May 31, 2013.

66. British Traitors: Ben Macintyre, *A Spy Among Friends: Kim Philby and the Great Betrayal* (2014), pp. 148-155; Daniel Silva, *The Other Woman* (2018), pp. 188-192, 365, 401-404.

67. Tripped up for Overbilling: Eugene L. Meyer, "Spy Game," *Bethesda Magazine*, September-October, 2011.

68. Spying for Castro: Toby Harnden, "Spying for Fidel: The Inside Story of Kendall and Gwen Myers," *The Washingtonian*, October 5, 2009; Tracey Eaton, "Espionage: The Myers case 10 years later," Cuba Money Project, June 18, 2019; Jim Popkin, "Ana Montes did much harm spying for Cuba. Chances are, you haven't heard of her." *Washington Post*, April 18, 2013; "Jennifer Miles: Master Spy," *San Francisco Chronicle*, October 24, 1970; Wallace and Melton, *Spy Sites of Washington, DC*, pp. 179-180, 240-241.

69. Sleeper Agent: *"The Americans"* created by Joe Weisberg for the FX television network, 2013-2018; Rosa Cartagena, "The DC Spy Sites You Walk by Every Day," *Washingtonian*, March 9, 2017; Gordon Corera, *Russians Among Us; Sleeper Cells, Ghost Stories and the Hunt for Putin's Spies* (2020) pp. 15, 209-211, 307, 385.

70. Russian redhead: Corera, *Russians Among Us*, pp. 375-376; James Bamford, "The Spy Who Wasn't," *The New Republic*, February 11, 2019; Sara Murray, "How the case against Maria Butina began to crumble," CNN, April 26, 2019; "Maria Butina: New job offered to agent deported from US," BBC, November 19, 2019.

Index

Harding, Florence, 28
Harding, Warren G., 28
Hayes, Rutherford B., 18
Heaton, Arthur, 102
Helm, Judith Beck, vii, 3, 5, 7, 8, 10, 13, 16, 46, 124, 125, 126
Henderson, Michele, 97
Henson, Jim, 70
Highlands estate, 57
Hiss, Alger, 110
Holder, Eric, 52
Holmes, Oliver Wendell, 4
Holmes, William Henry, 2
Hoover, Herbert, 58
Hoover, J. Edgar, 44
Hope Diamond, 29
Hopkins, Harry, 109
House of Sweden, 103
Hubbard, Gardiner Greene, 92
Humphrey, Hubert, 53
Huntley, Chet, 71
Hurst, John Fletcher, 34

Illuminati, 27
Immaculata Seminary, 10, 38
India, 29, 39, 68, 113
Indigenous (people), v, 2, 4, 41, 124
International Chancery Center, 23, 84, 85, 88, 90
International Monetary Fund, 96, 122
Iran, 11, 62, 85
Israel, 39, 49, 84, 88, 89, 113

Jamaica, 97
Jefferson, Thomas, 6, 27, 78
Jeju, 42
Jesse Reno School, ii, 16
Johns Hopkins University, 115, 116
Johnson, Lyndon, 52, 53
Jones, Alex, 80
Jordan, 84

Kamalananda, 68
Karuna, 68
Katzen, Cyrus, 44
Kelman, Jim, 99
Kenji, grandson, 25
Kennedy, David M., 31
Kennedy, Jackie, 53
Kennedy, John F., 39, 53, 60, 70
Kent, Julie, 65
Kermit the Frog, 70
Key, Francis Scott, 17
KGB, 94, 110, 117
Khomeini, Ali, 11
Khrushchev, Nikita, 55
King, Jr, Martin Luther, 22

Kissinger, Henry, 56
Knox, John, 74
Korean, 36, 42, 43, 49
Korean War, 99
Kremlin, 94, 95, 121
Kristin, cousin, 58, 123
Kushner, Jared, 84
Kuwait, 84
Kyoko, wife, 36, 42, 91, 101, 123

Lafayette, Marquis de, 78
Landingham, Mrs., 22
Lawrence, David F., 102
Le Carré, John, 112
Lee Dai-Won, 99
Lee, Robert E., 14
Leno, Jay, 118
Letelier, Orlando, 41
Lewis, Michael, 23
Library of Congress, ii
Lincoln, Abraham, 13, 31
Liu, Xiaobo, 90
Longworth, Alice Roosevelt, 28
López Obrador, Andrés Manuel, 105
Loughborough, Nathan, 71
Louis XVI, 29
Lyons, Harold, 24

Maclean, Donald, 110, 111
Madison, James, 6
Malaysia, 84
Manning, Rebecca, 112
Mansfield, Mike, 62
Marie Antoinette, 29
mason. See Freemasonry
Mason, Roy, 76, 127
Mattis, Jim, 22
McCarthy, Eugene, 60
McCarthy, Joseph, 121
McLean Gardens, 28, 29, 120
McLean, Edward (Ned) Beale, 28, 29
McLean, John R., 28
Meet the Press, 71
Mesta, Perle, 53
Metro, ii, 7, 9, 20, 30, 53
Mexican Cultural Institute, 105
Mexico, 105
Miles, Jennifer, 116
Miller Development Company, 48, 52
Miranda, Lin-Manuel, 6, 122, 124
Montes, Ana Belén, 116
Morocco, 84
Moscow, 29, 94, 112, 119, 121
Mossad, 114
Mount Alban, 60
Mount Alto, 56, 94, 95

Works Progress Administration (WPA), 109
World Bank, 122
World Future Society, 76
World Health Organization, 91
World War I, 45, 48
World War II, 21, 25, 28, 54, 60, 62, 66, 67, 73, 84,
   93, 107
Wormley, James, 17, 18
Wormley's Hotel, 17, 18
Xanadu house, 76

Yamaguchi, Tamon, 61
Yamamoto, Isoroku, 61
Yemen, 104
Yoshida, Isoya, 100
Yuma Study Center, 54

Zhao, Lijian, 90
Zouaves, 13, 124
Zumwalt, Jim, 62, 123